OCCASIONAL PAPER 194

Fiscal and Macroeconomic Impact of Privatization

Jeffrey Davis, Rolando Ossowski,
Thomas Richardson, and Steven Barnett

INTERNATIONAL MONETARY FUND
Washington DC
2000

Production: IMF Graphics Section
Typesetting: Julio R. Prego
Figures: Sanaa Elaroussi

Library of Congress Cataloging-in-Publication Data

Fiscal and macroeconomic impact of privatization / Jeffrey Davis... [et al.].
p. cm—(Occasional paper, ISSN 0251-6365 ; no. 194)

Includes bibliographical references.
ISBN 1-55775-888-3

   1. Privatization—Case studies.   2. Government business enterprises—
Case studies.   3. Finance, Public—Case studies.   I. Davis, Jeffrey M.,
1946   II. Occasional paper (International Monetary Fund) ; 194.
HD3845.6 .F57 2000
338.9'25—dc21   00-0031909

Price: US$20.00
(US$17.50 to full-time faculty members and
students at universities and colleges)

Please send orders to:
International Monetary Fund, Publication Services
700 19th Street, N.W., Washington, D.C. 20431, U.S.A.
Tel.: (202) 623-7430   Telefax: (202) 623-7201
E-mail: publications@imf.org
Internet: http://www.imf.org

recycled paper

Contents

Boxes

Section

Tables

Section

Figures

Section

The following symbols have been used throughout this paper:

. . . to indicate that data are not available;

n.a. to indicate not applicable;

— to indicate that the figure is zero or less than half the final digit shown, or that the item does not exist;

– between years or months (i.e., 1997–98 or January–June) to indicate the years or months covered, including the beginning and ending years or months;

/ between years or months (i.e., 1997/98) to indicate a crop or fiscal (financial) year.

"Billion" means a thousand million; "trillion" means a thousand billion.

Minor discrepancies between constituent figures and totals are due to rounding.

The term "country," as used in this paper, does not in all cases refer to a territorial entity that is a state as understood by international law and practice; the term also covers some territorial entities that are not states, but for which statistical data are maintained and provided internationally on a separate and independent basis.

Preface

The paper reflects the contributions of several members of staff in the IMF's Fiscal Affairs Department. In particular, the authors are grateful to Rosa Alonso, Benedict Bingham, Isaias Coelho, Louis Kuijs, Jun Ma, Eric Mottu, Martin Petri, Arnim Schwidrowski, István Székely, George Tsibouris, and Timo Välilä for their research into the privatization experience of the case study countries. They would also like to thank John Nellis, as well as others at the World Bank, for their advice and support. Helpful and insightful comments on the paper were provided by Vito Tanzi, and colleagues in the Fiscal Affairs Department and in other departments in the IMF.

The authors appreciate as well the efficient research assistance provided by William Riordan and the document preparation assistance provided by Heather Huckstep. Gail Berre of the External Relations Department edited the paper and coordinated production of the publication.

The views expressed in the paper, as well as any errors, are the sole responsibility of the authors and do not necessarily represent the opinions of the Executive Board of the IMF or other members of the IMF staff.

1 Overview

Privatization has been a key element of structural reform in many developing and transition economies during the last decade. Governments undertaking privatization have pursued a variety of objectives: achieving gains in economic efficiency, given the extensive prevalence of poor economic performance of public enterprises in many countries and limited success with their reform; and improving the fiscal position, particularly in cases where governments have been unwilling or unable to continue to finance deficits in the public enterprise sector. In addition, liquidity-constrained governments facing fiscal pressures have sometimes privatized with a view to financing fiscal deficits with the proceeds. Other objectives have included the development of domestic capital markets.

These efforts have been reviewed in a large literature on the microeconomic aspects of privatization that has emphasized the potential efficiency gains. However, there has been less work, particularly of an empirical nature, done on the fiscal and macroeconomic impact of privatization.[1] Among the international financial institutions, the World Bank has had the lead role in advising on the design and implementation of the reform of public enterprises, including divestiture. Privatization, however, has important fiscal and macroeconomic implications and is therefore also of interest to the International Monetary Fund (IMF). Indeed, privatization has become an important component of programs in a large number of countries.

This paper reviews fiscal and macroeconomic issues in the privatization of nonfinancial public enterprises in developing and transition economies.[2] Suc-cessive sections of the paper consider the following issues: proceeds from privatization and the factors determining the amount accruing to the budget; uses of the proceeds; empirical evidence on the impact of privatization on the budget and macroeconomic aggregates; and the privatization component of IMF-supported programs. The empirical evidence draws on a series of case study countries selected to be representative of a range of privatization experience in developing and transition economies and to reflect geographical diversity.[3]

Privatization Proceeds

Proceeds from privatization have been substantial in a number of developing and transition economies. Gross receipts that can be transferred to the budget are affected by actions prior to sale, the sales process, and the postprivatization regime. Amounts accruing to the budget are found to be less than the sales proceeds as a result of extrabudgetary management and the wide divergence between gross and net receipts. Among the major conclusions concerning privatization proceeds are the following:

First, off-budget placement of privatization proceeds can lead to limited control and lack of transparency in their use. *Extrabudgetary funds* should be regulated, with accounts publicly reported, audited, and subject to parliamentary oversight.

Second, privatization transactions should be transparently reported on a *gross basis*. Costs for restructuring, recapitalization, or writing off public enterprise debt should be recorded as spending financed by the gross proceeds of sale.

Third, privatization is an exchange of assets; the receipts are lumpy, one-off, and uncertain. Thus, *privatization proceeds should be treated as a financing item* in the fiscal accounts.

---

[1]An excellent survey of the microeconomic literature is provided in Megginson and Netter (1999). Heller (1990) and Hemming and Mansoor (1987) provide examples of earlier discussions of fiscal and macroeconomic issues, and Hachette and Lüders (1993), Pinheiro and Schneider (1995), and Larraín and Winograd (1996) offer examples of more recent empirical work in this area. World Bank (1995) discusses many aspects of international privatization experience.

[2]For a discussion of issues in the privatization of financial institutions, see Beyer, Dziobek, and Garrett (1999); and Verbrugge, Megginson, and Owens (1999).

[3]The sample comprises 18 countries and includes 10 nontransition economies (Argentina, Bolivia, Côte d'Ivoire, Egypt, Mexico, Morocco, Mozambique, Peru, the Philippines, and Uganda) and 8 transition economies (the Czech Republic, Estonia, Hungary, Kazakhstan, Mongolia, Russia, Ukraine, and Vietnam).

Uses of Privatization Proceeds

An evaluation of the potential uses of privatization receipts should reflect the implications for government net worth and their macroeconomic impact.

Insofar as *government net worth* is concerned, receipts from privatization do not of themselves indicate that the government is better off. Privatization has longer-term implications in terms of revenues foregone and/or expenditures that will not be made in the future, and government decisions on the use of proceeds should reflect these intertemporal effects. Government net worth will rise to the extent that private sector ownership leads to an increase in efficiency and the government shares in this gain.

The *macroeconomic effects* of privatization depend, in part, on whether receipts are from domestic or foreign sources, the degree of capital mobility, and the exchange regime. Broadly, the effects of an increase in the deficit financed by privatization receipts would be similar to those resulting from a debt-financed fiscal expansion. Use of proceeds to reduce external debt provides for an automatic sterilization of what may be substantial capital inflows associated with privatization. Reduction of domestic debt may impact domestic liquidity.

Assessment of governments' stated intentions with respect to the use of privatization receipts needs to allow for the fungibility of resources. Uses commonly considered are

- *Higher expenditure.* Privatization receipts are temporary and often uncertain, thus it is not advisable to rely on them for current spending. Targeted use to help cushion the short-term social impact of privatization can be appropriate. Use of the proceeds to finance additional capital spending need not reduce government net worth, though it often raises concerns as to the quality of the projects.
- *Reduction in net debt.* This may be achieved by retiring debt (or settling arrears), or building up assets, with the choice determined by debt management considerations. Advantages include maintenance of government net worth and possibly favorable signaling effects that could impact the cost and availability of debt.
- *Earmarking of privatization receipts.* Doing so for particular expenditures complicates fiscal management and makes it difficult to reallocate spending in response to changes in circumstances and priorities. As such it should be discouraged.
- *Relaxing the fiscal constraint.* Privatization proceeds might serve a limited role in providing a temporary cushion for countries pursuing aggressive adjustment and reform programs.

Fiscal Impact of Privatization

Privatization has a contemporaneous impact on the budget and budgetary effects over time. Econometric results suggest that, for the case study countries, *privatization receipts are saved rather than spent.* This result applies for receipts channeled through the budget, which does not support arguments that extrabudgetary treatment is necessarily required for prudent management. Most of the countries covered had an IMF program in place, and consequent limitations on the deficit may have substantially influenced this finding.

Piecemeal evidence suggests that, over time, *the fiscal situation tends to benefit from privatization.* In particular, both the firm level and more aggregate data support positive impacts on revenue; transfers decline markedly following periods of privatization; and broader indicators of consolidated public enterprise accounts for some countries indicate a large decline in deficits, and probably also in quasi-fiscal operations.

Data on public enterprise operations and on the financial flows between enterprises and the government (including quasi-fiscal flows) are often inadequate. There is a need for improvements in this area in many countries.

Macroeconomic Impact of Privatization

Both the microeconomic and case study data are supportive of the positive effects of privatization over time on growth and employment. These results hold for the full sample and the transition countries, though they are less pronounced for the latter.

Growth

The microeconomic evidence indicates that private firms are operationally more efficient than those held by the state, particularly in competitive industries. A strong correlation is also found for the case study countries between privatization and growth. However, and consistent with the growth literature, privatization is likely serving as a proxy in the regressions for one or more missing variables that may broadly be characterized as a favorable regime change.

Labor Markets

Public enterprises often seek to maintain employment, and benefit from soft budget constraints. Consequently, there is concern that privatization may lead to increased unemployment. Although empirical evidence suggests that aggregate unemployment tends to decrease following privatization, particular groups of workers may still be adversely affected. This lends importance to measures that mitigate its social impact.

Issues for IMF-Supported Programs

The World Bank takes the lead in privatization, but the IMF has cooperated closely with it in this area. Drawing on the Bank's experience and recommendations, a majority of IMF-supported programs in recent years have included some form of conditionality on privatization.

Monitoring of privatization in IMF-supported programs has emphasized conditionality on process and targets. Consistent with the recent emphasis in the World Bank, there is scope for IMF conditionality to give more weight to privatization procedures where these have important fiscal and macroeconomic impact. Similarly, programs should, in some cases, give greater importance to the establishment of an appropriate regulatory environment within which privatized firms operate.

The *design of financial programs* should include as broad a definition of privatization receipts as possible in the fiscal targets and quantitative performance criteria, and consider the macroeconomic effects in assessing use. Adjusters should address the uncertainty attached to the amount of receipts; in general, higher-than-anticipated receipts should be saved.

II   Privatization Proceeds

This section presents data on the scale of gross privatization proceeds and the amounts accruing to the budget for the case study countries. It then considers the factors affecting budgetary proceeds and their treatment in the fiscal accounts.

Scale of Privatization Proceeds in the Case Study Countries

Table 1 presents data on gross privatization receipts and the amounts accruing to the budget. Data on cumulative gross privatization proceeds collected during the years of active privatization through 1997 are derived from a privatization database prepared by the World Bank. Privatization proceeds were on average 1¾ percent of GDP a year during the active privatization period. For the transition case study countries, this figure was 2 percent of GDP a year, while for nontransition countries it was 1½ percent of GDP.[4]

A somewhat different picture is provided, however, by data on privatization proceeds accruing to the budget as recorded in the IMF's fiscal accounts. These proceeds were on average ¾ percent of GDP a year during the active privatization period (see Table 1 and Table 2). It is striking that in many countries the privatization proceeds actually received by the budget were less, and in some cases significantly so, than the gross privatization receipts. The institutional, operational, and accounting reasons for these differences are discussed in the next section.

Factors Affecting Budgetary Proceeds

Gross receipts that can be transferred to the budget are affected by actions prior to sale, the sales process, and the postprivatization regime. In some countries, these receipts have been limited by invest-

ments to physically restructure public enterprises prior to privatization, restrictions on potential bidders, and postprivatization commitments on the new owners.[5] Actions in those various areas may also give rise to governance issues. Factors affecting the sale price of assets are reviewed in Appendix I.

As noted above, in many countries the budgetary proceeds from privatization have been less than the gross sales value of the assets divested. This reflects extrabudgetary management of the privatization proceeds and the fact that budgets have tended to receive the net value of divested assets after certain costs have been subtracted.

Extrabudgetary Management of Privatization Proceeds

From an institutional point of view, privatization revenues may accrue in the first instance to the budget or to off-budget public institutions. The case study countries illustrate the prevalence of off-budget treatment of privatization transactions (see Table 3). In several cases, the proceeds initially accrued to an extrabudgetary fund, which then made transfers to the budget of a portion of the receipts. In a few instances, the proceeds are recorded entirely off budget. These institutional and operational arrangements may have reflected two concerns on the part of governments: first, the notion that privatization proceeds should be held off budget as a means of protecting them from parliaments that might be inclined to spend them inappropriately; and second, the one-off nature of privatization proceeds and the perception that they constitute an unexpected windfall.

The accrual of privatization receipts to off-budget agencies and/or their exclusion from the budget may hamper fiscal policy control and reduce transparency and oversight. Although in some countries the financial transactions related to extrabudgetary

---

[4]These data underestimate the extent of state divestiture of assets to the extent that noncash methods of privatization—such as vouchers in transition countries—were used.

[5]Appropriate regulatory frameworks should, however, be set up prior to the privatization of public enterprises with substantial monopoly power.

Table 1. Gross and Budgetary Privatization Proceeds in Case Study Countries

	Years of Active Privatization	Gross Privatization Proceeds During Period of Active Privatization[1]		Net Privatization Proceeds Accruing to Budget During Period of Active Privatization[2]		Ratio of Net Proceeds Accruing to Budget to Gross Proceeds[3]
		Millions of U.S. dollars	Percent of GDP[4]	Millions of U.S. dollars[5]	Percent of GDP[4]	Percent
Argentina	1990–95	22,885	2.0	11,452	0.9	50
Bolivia	1995–98	863	4.2	160	0.5	12
Côte d'Ivoire	1994–97	459	1.1	448	1.1	98
Czech Republic	1991–97	2,369	0.9	1,736	0.8	73
Egypt	1993–98	2,778	0.8	2,194	0.5	79
Estonia	1992–98	467	2.9	—	—	—
Hungary	1991–98	11,841	4.0	6,672	2.2	56
Kazakhstan	1993–98	5,798	5.5	2,425	2.2	25
Mexico	1989–94	25,249	1.3	6,310	0.3	25
Mongolia	1994–98	…	…	45	0.9	…
Morocco	1993–97	1,489	1.0	1,307	0.9	88
Mozambique	1992–98	101	1.1	—	—	—
Peru	1994–97	7,136	3.2	5,821	2.6	82
Philippines	1987–97	3,810	0.7	3,407	0.5	88
Russia	1992–98	6,569	0.3	8,632	0.4	…
Uganda	1991–98	152	0.4	—	—	—
Ukraine	1993–98	24	—	518	0.2	…
Vietnam	1993–98	3	—	—	—	—
Average of all countries with data		n.a.	1.7	n.a.	0.8	45
Average of transition countries with data[6]		n.a.	1.9	n.a.	0.8	31
Average of nontransition countries with data[7]		n.a.	1.6	n.a.	0.7	52

Sources: World Bank; and IMF staff estimates.

[1] World Bank Privatization database. Data are available for 1988–97.

[2] Executive Board documents and staff estimates. Data through latest available observation.

[3] Ratio calculated for the period of active privatization for which information is available in both sets of data. Differences in coverage in the two series may account for the higher proceeds recorded in IMF data for Russia and Ukraine.

[4] Average of annual ratios of privatization proceeds to GDP during the period of active privatization. For the Philippines, ratios to GNP.

[5] Annual data in national currency converted to U.S. dollars using annual average exchange rates.

[6] Transition case study countries comprise the Czech Republic, Estonia, Hungary, Kazakhstan, Mongolia, Russia, Ukraine, and Vietnam.

[7] Nontransition case study countries comprise Argentina, Bolivia, Côte d'Ivoire, Egypt, Mexico, Morocco, Mozambique, Peru, the Philippines, and Uganda.

funds—including those with responsibility for privatization and state enterprise management—are transparent and subject to parliamentary or other oversight (for instance, in Hungary), this is not always the case. The privatization receipts that do not flow through the budget may then be subject to less public scrutiny on their accrual and use than regular budgetary spending.[6] In addition, the use of the proceeds may not be subject to priority-setting within the budget process.

_____
[6]Section 2.1.1 of the *Code of Good Practices on Fiscal Transparency—Declaration of Principles* states: "The annual budget should cover all central government operations in detail and should also provide information on central government extrabudgetary activities."

In Uganda, for example, privatization receipts were placed off budget in a "divestiture account," which was charged with paying off the debts of public enterprises, compensating workers who were laid off as a result of divestiture, and other unspecified purposes meant to promote successful privatization. The legislation setting up the divestiture account was vague on accounting and audit procedures, and allegations of misuse of the funds that passed through it—as well as widespread asset-stripping— have led to frequent complaints by parliament, among others, that governance issues in the privatization process needed to be addressed.

Privatization proceeds should be transparently recorded and subject to effective oversight. This

Table 2. Privatization Proceeds Accruing to the Budget in Case Study Countries[1]

(In percent of GDP)

	1990	1991	1992	1993	1994	1995	1996	1997	1998	Annual Average During Active Privatization Period[2]
Argentina	1.0	1.2	0.8	1.5	0.3	0.4	0.1	—	—	0.9
Bolivia	0.1	0.1	0.2	—	0.2	0.2	0.3	0.9	0.6	0.5
Côte d'Ivoire	...	...	0.1	0.1	0.2	0.7	1.0	2.4	0.5	1.1
Czech Republic	...	...	...	0.7	1.4	1.2	0.2	0.4	—	0.8
Egypt[3]	...	...	...	—	—	—	0.2	2.5	...	0.5
Estonia	...	—	—	—	—	—	—	—	—	—
Hungary	...	0.4	1.5	1.0	1.7	4.0	4.2	2.6	...	2.2
Kazakhstan	...	...	...	2.7	0.3	0.7	2.2	3.3	4.3	2.2
Mexico	—	0.3	0.8	0.4	0.2	—	—	0.6	0.4	0.3
Mongolia	...	...	...	—	0.2	0.9	0.4	1.4	1.7	0.9
Morocco[3]	—	—	—	0.9	0.7	0.4	1.0	1.4	0.4	0.9
Mozambique	—	—	—	—	—	—	—	—	...	—
Peru	...	—	0.1	0.4	4.6	1.6	3.3	0.9	0.4	2.6
Philippines[4]	0.3	0.3	0.1	0.1	1.7	1.2	0.3	0.4	0.1	0.5
Russia	...	...	0.5	0.2	0.1	0.3	0.1	0.9	0.7	0.4
Uganda[3]	...	—	—	—	—	—	—	—	—	—
Ukraine	...	...	...	0.1	0.2	0.1	0.2	0.1	0.4	0.2
Vietnam	...	...	...	—	—	—	—	—	—	—
Average of all countries with data	0.3	0.2	0.3	0.5	0.7	0.7	0.8	1.0	0.6	0.8
Average of all transition countries with data[5]	...	0.2	0.7	0.6	0.5	0.9	0.9	1.1	1.0	0.8
Average of all nontransition countries with data[6]	0.3	0.2	0.2	0.3	0.8	0.5	0.6	0.9	0.3	0.7

Source: IMF staff estimates.

[1]Shaded years indicate periods of active privatization.

[2]Average of annual ratios of privatization proceeds to GDP during the period of active privatization.

[3]Data for Egypt, Morocco, and Uganda are on a fiscal year basis, shown in the table as the year in which the fiscal year begins. In 1996, Morocco switched from a January–December fiscal year to a July–June fiscal year. As a result, 1996 data are for the first half of 1996 only, 1997 data are for July 1996–June 1997, and 1998 data are for July 1997–June 1998.

[4]In percent of GNP.

[5]Transition case study countries comprise the Czech Republic, Estonia, Hungary, Kazakhstan, Mongolia, Russia, Ukraine, and Vietnam.

[6]Nontransition case study countries comprise Argentina, Bolivia, Côte d'Ivoire, Egypt, Mexico, Morocco, Mozambique, Peru, the Philippines, and Uganda.

could be achieved through full consolidation of the privatization accounts in the budget that is approved by parliament to ensure that the claim on government resources arising from privatization expenses, as well as the revenues, are adequately accounted for; that financing decisions are taken with due regard to all government assets and liabilities; and that all operations affecting the government's balance sheet are reported to parliament. If, however, extrabudgetary institutions are in charge of privatization, their operations must be subject to clear rules and regulations, and they should be publicly reported, audited, and subject to parliamentary oversight. Consolidated general government fiscal performance, inclusive of privatization transactions, should also be reported.

Reporting Gross Versus Net Privatization Proceeds

In virtually all of the case study countries, privatization proceeds were reported on a net basis (in both the IMF and the authorities' accounts), after taking account of the overhead costs of the privatization agency, and usually after subtracting the costs of any preprivatization restructuring. Moreover, it is difficult to form an accurate picture of the overall gross amount of sales proceeds, and relatively little information is available on the actual disposition of the assets that were allocated to the costs of privatization.

In many cases, only cash privatization revenues are included in the budgetary or fiscal accounts. Payments made by buyers in the form of debt instruments previously issued by the government selling the assets have often not been included in the privatization revenues reported in the fiscal accounts. Since payment in the form of government debt instruments represents amortization of public debt, a clearer picture is conveyed by including in the privatization receipts the market value of the debt extinguished, and by showing debt amortization as counterpart.

These considerations suggest that a transparent approach to recording the transactions related to disposing of state assets would be on a gross basis. This would involve reporting expenditures for restructuring, recapitalization, or for writing off public enterprise debt as expenditures on the budget that are financed by the gross proceeds of the sales.[7]

Fiscal Reporting of Privatization Proceeds

The accounting treatment of privatization proceeds does not itself predetermine use. However, the way that privatization receipts are presented in the fiscal accounts may have a bearing on decisions regarding their use, as well as on public perceptions of the fiscal stance.

This issue involves the question of whether such proceeds should be regarded as government revenue or as financing. The current version of *A Manual on Government Finance Statistics* (IMF, 1986) takes the position that transactions involving nonfinancial assets are part of capital revenue or expenditure, and that financial asset transactions undertaken for policy purposes are part of net lending. Hence, it recommends that privatization receipts be treated as a deficit-determining ("above-the-line") item and recorded as capital revenue in the case of sales of equipment, and (negative) net lending in the case of shares. The suggested classification ensures consistency in the intertemporal treatment of the assets in

question. If the acquisition of the productive asset or original investment in the public enterprise were undertaken for policy purposes and classified as deficit-determining items, on grounds of symmetry a similar treatment would be required in the case of privatization proceeds.

This treatment of receipts from the sale of assets has been regarded as an unsatisfactory basis for fiscal analysis for some time. Privatization receipts have characteristics that warrant differentiating them from other government revenues in the design and assessment of fiscal policy: privatization is an exchange of assets, and spending the proceeds affects the government's intertemporal budget constraint; these receipts represent one-off resources and should not be counted upon to support the fiscal position permanently; their lumpy nature can distort analysis of the underlying deficit and provide a misleading view of the sustainability of the fiscal position; and, in general they are more uncertain in timing and size than other government revenues. Because of these considerations, it is preferable to treat privatization proceeds as a financing ("below-the-line") item in the fiscal accounts (Mackenzie, 1998).

A revision of *A Manual on Government Finance Statistics* is under way, which will address the problems in the treatment of privatization proceeds by clearly separating asset/liability transactions from government operations that change net worth. Also, a distinction will be made between asset/liability transactions that are undertaken for policy purposes and those intended to manage the liquidity position of the government. In this new treatment, privatization proceeds will have no impact on the balance of government operations that determines the change in net worth, but the proceeds will be a determinant of the volume of transactions required for managing the government's liquidity position.

In most of the case study countries, the proceeds from privatization that go through the budget were classified above the line by the authorities, either as revenue or as negative net lending. The fiscal accounts compiled by IMF staff for the countries in the sample, however, increasingly record privatization receipts as an element of deficit financing; currently, this is done in about two-thirds of the cases in the sample (see Table 3).

---

[7]If the amount of public enterprise liabilities assumed by the budget is large, it might be appropriate to show a deficit including and excluding this amount.

Table 3. Budgetary Treatment and Classification of Privatization Proceeds

Country	Placement of Proceeds	Official Budgetary Recording and Classification	IMF Budget Classification
Argentina	Budget	On budget: revenue	Financing
Bolivia	Capitalization: enterprise	Capitalization part: off budget	
	Cash receipts: budget	Cash receipts: on budget: revenue	Cash receipts: revenue[1]
Côte d'Ivoire	Budget	On budget: revenue[2]	Financing
Czech Republic	Agency[3]	On budget: lending minus repayment[4]	Revenue[4]
Egypt	Agency[3]	Only transfers from agency: financing	Financing[5]
Estonia	Agency (partly)[6]	Agency part: off budget	Financing (since 1999)[7]
	Budget (partly)	Budget part: revenue	Not included (through 1998)
Hungary	Agency[3]	Only transfers from agency: revenue	Financing (since 1998)[5]
			Revenue (through 1997)[5]
Kazakhstan	Budget	On budget: lending minus repayment	Financing (since 1998)
			Revenue (through 1997)
Mexico	Budget (partly)	Revenue[8]	Revenue[8]
Mongolia	Budget	On budget: revenue	Revenue
Morocco	Budget	On budget: revenue	Financing[9]
Mozambique	Agency[6]	Off budget	Revenue (since 1999)
			Not included (through 1998)
Peru	Budget (partly)	On budget: revenue[10]	Financing (since 1996)
			Revenue (through 1995)
Philippines	Budget	On budget: revenue	Financing (since 1998)
			Revenue (through 1997)
Russia	Budget	On budget: revenue	Financing
Uganda	Agency[6]	Off budget	Not included
Ukraine	Budget	On budget: revenue	Financing
Vietnam	Agency[6]	Off budget	Not included

Sources: Data provided by country authorities; and IMF staff.

[1]Under Bolivia's capitalization scheme, investors bid for a 50 percent stake in the public enterprise in exchange for a commitment to undertake investment. The remaining shareholding is retained by the government and used to finance a minimum pension scheme. The capitalization program is treated as off-budget investment in the firms partly divested.

[2]In the official classification, all financing is treated as "revenue."

[3]The privatization agency makes transfers to the budget.

[4]The revenue accruing to the privatization agency is consolidated in the budget and in the IMF budget accounts since 1998. The fiscal balance is shown including and excluding privatization receipts.

[5]Only includes the privatization proceeds transferred to the government by the privatization agencies.

[6]The privatization agency does not make transfers to the budget.

[7]Only the part accruing to the budget.

[8]Proceeds from the privatization of Telmex and commercial banks were kept off budget.

[9]Recorded on a separate line in the IMF presentation between the overall balance (excluding privatization receipts) and financing.

[10]Proceeds used for social expenditure and to recapitalize the pension fund were kept off budget. The Ministry of Finance shows budgetary proceeds as revenue, and the central bank as financing.

III Use of Privatization Proceeds

The appropriate size of the fiscal deficit is largely determined by the overall macroeconomic objectives and fiscal sustainability. Viewed as a source of financing, akin to a bond sale, the amount of privatization proceeds generally should not itself determine the size of the deficit, and, moreover, the macroeconomic consequences are also similar to conventional bond financing. Nonetheless, privatization proceeds are distinct in certain ways. First, privatization may impact government net worth, which in turn has consequences for fiscal sustainability. Second, the privatization program might pose specific risks to macroeconomic stability—partly due to the size, lumpiness, and uncertain timing of privatization receipts—that enhance the need for monetary and fiscal policy coordination. And third, the discrete nature of privatization proceeds leads to questions regarding their appropriate use.

Privatization and Government Net Worth

The privatization of government productive assets yields immediate financial proceeds. But the receipts from privatization do not of themselves indicate that the government is better off or that its spending constraints today and over time are relaxed. Privatization has longer-term implications in terms of revenues foregone and/or expenditures that will not be made in the future, and government decisions on the use of privatization proceeds should reflect these intertemporal effects. Assessing them requires an analysis of the impact of privatization on the income flows and on government net worth.

The financial relationship between the government and public enterprises includes budgetary receipts of taxes and dividends, and other transfers from, and current or capital transfers to, public enterprises, including in the form of subsidies. In addition, there are often quasi-fiscal costs that are not recorded in the budget, such as directed and/or subsidized lending, as well as contingent liabilities associated with implicit or explicit government guarantees. The analysis of intrapublic sector financial flows should also consider any cross arrears, for instance, arrears on utility bills by the government and other public sector entities, which are common in some countries.

In a broader context, therefore, the change in government net worth due to privatization would equal the sum of the privatization proceeds and the net present value of the taxes of the privatized firm, minus the sum of the net present value of the net subsidies and transfers (including dividends) to or from the public enterprise (including quasi-fiscal costs)[8] and the net present value of the lost taxes of the public enterprise.[9]

In the case where the rate of return on the asset in the public sector equals that of the asset in private hands, the government receives financial assets and gives up a stream of net future earnings on the assets of equal value. Privatization in this case would simply involve a change in the composition of the government's assets without effects on its net worth, and the government's intertemporal budget constraint would not be affected. However, the conditions for this to be true are restrictive: markets should be efficient—meaning, among other things, that informational asymmetries should not be important and that the government can privatize efficiently; the public and private sectors must use the same discount rate; the firm should be no more or less profitable after privatization; and it should face an identical external environment before and after privatization (Heller, 1990, and Hemming and Mansoor, 1987).

If the private sector is expected to run the enterprise more efficiently than would the state, government net worth would increase provided the government can privatize and tax efficiently. In such a case, the government's intertemporal budget constraint

---

[8]This assumes that such transfers cease after privatization.

[9]The sale of a productive asset, which would have yielded a certain rate of return in the form of dividends or social benefits had it remained in public hands, may be compared to that of a government bond. In either case, the state receives liquid assets that, were they to be used to finance current expenditures, would require higher taxes or lower spending in the future. However, the one-off nature of privatization is an important feature that distinguishes it from the issuance of bonds.

would be loosened, and privatization would have a permanent effect on public finances. Conversely, the sale price of a public enterprise may be below the net present value of the expected flow of net earnings in private hands: the state, which may manage a firm less efficiently than would the private sector, may not be capable of selling it well either; it may choose to sell the firm at a price less than the maximum in recognition of externalities associated with the creation and development of capital markets; and the private and the public sector may value a firm differently due to different tolerances for risk, access to financial markets, and rates of time preference. Moreover, a government facing liquidity constraints may be willing to sell state assets at less than their economic value to finance higher expenditure.

Short-run Macroeconomic Effects of Privatization

Decisions on the use of privatization receipts should reflect the consequent impact on the fiscal policy stance and on macroeconomic aggregates and objectives. These implications may differ according to such factors as the source of privatization receipts (domestic or external), the degree of capital mobility, and the exchange rate regime. It is also important to consider the fiscal and monetary policy implications of the substantial capital inflows that may be linked to privatization.

Fiscal Stance

The effects of an increase in the deficit through higher spending or lower taxes that is financed by privatization proceeds would be similar to those resulting from a fiscal expansion financed by an increase in public debt (Mackenzie, 1998). It would put pressure on domestic demand with consequences for activity, inflation, and the external current account. The relative significance of these effects will depend in part on the initial macroeconomic position and the composition of the increase in spending in terms of imported and domestic goods and services.

The effects of a fiscal expansion financed with privatization proceeds will, in many developing countries, depend on the source of the proceeds, though this need not be the case with perfect capital mobility.[10] If the receipts are from abroad, the ef-

fects would be similar to a foreign-financed increase in the fiscal deficit and are likely to include pressure toward the real appreciation of the currency. For domestic receipts, the impact on aggregate demand would be similar to that of an expansion financed with domestic bond placements. In this case, the need for the buyer to finance the purchase could put upward pressure on interest rates, and the effect on aggregate demand may be more limited.[11]

The government may use privatization proceeds to reduce its net indebtedness by retiring external or domestic debt, settling domestic or external arrears (if any), building up financial assets at home or abroad, or depositing the proceeds with the central bank. These operations would generally be associated with reductions in the country's risk premium. An automatic sterilization of foreign privatization receipts is achieved by parallel reductions in the net public external debt, including domestic currency debt held by nonresidents and external arrears. The external current account benefits from such operations and the reduction of country risk through lower net public interest payments. This, however, will be offset, at least in part, by remittances of profits and dividends to foreign investors holding shares in privatized firms.

In some countries, privatization proceeds may, in part, be used to repay domestic debt, particularly when this debt is expensive and the external debt is mainly on concessional terms. Consideration needs to be given, however, to the effects on domestic liquidity and interest rates of a net redemption of government domestic debt, including foreign currency debt held by residents and domestic arrears, under conditions of less-than-perfect capital mobility. This could be expansionary, including through the associated reduction in interest rates, and might imply the need for offsetting monetary policy measures.

Privatization and Capital Inflows

Large-scale privatization programs have sometimes been associated with capital inflows that have created complications for macroeconomic policy. Such inflows can pose challenges to financial policies if the government spends them or repays domestic debt. There is a direct link between privatization and capital inflows when asset sales are financed through foreign direct investment.[12] Additional capital inflows may occur in the form of foreign direct investment if the new owners of privat-

---

[10]If the source of the privatization receipts is domestic, the excess demand for money resulting from the purchase of the asset by the private sector would be expected to lead to capital inflows that would be similar to an inflow of privatization proceeds from abroad. However, this requires well-functioning domestic financial markets.

[11]The actual impact on interest rates will depend on the subsequent use of the proceeds and the degree of openness of the capital market.

[12]Estimates based on World Bank data suggest that, on average, close to 40 percent of privatization receipts were paid in foreign exchange in the case study countries.

Box 1. Sterilization of Privatization Revenues in Hungary

The Hungarian privatization process generated significant revenues in the years 1991–98, when gross privatization proceeds averaged 4 percent of GDP a year, largely from abroad. In the early 1990s, Hungary followed a fixed, but frequently adjusted, exchange rate, and in early 1995 the government switched to a crawling peg system. Under both regimes, the spending by the government of part of the privatization revenues, as well as capital flows associated with privatization, posed challenges to monetary policy. Capital inflows led to increases in the money supply, thereby potentially compromising the objectives for inflation (to the extent that the liquidity injection exceeded the growth in base money demand), and the real exchange rate. At various times, the authorities attempted to sterilize the effect of capital flows on monetary aggregates.

The challenges for monetary policy posed by privatization-related capital inflows, and government deficits partly financed with privatization receipts, first appeared in 1991, when significant foreign direct investment was received, while a decline of real GDP by more than 10 percent reduced money demand. This created pressure for the National Bank of Hungary to remove liquidity from the system through sterilization. In the next three years, as foreign direct investment flows continued—most of them related to privatization—while output remained subdued and inflation remained high, some sterilization took place through the issuance of interest-bearing debt. At the same time, the National Bank of Hungary used changes in reserve requirements to influence liquidity.

In 1995, in the aftermath of financial turmoil triggered by concerns over Hungary's capacity to service its foreign debt, the privatization process was speeded up as part of a stabilization package. The new government made the reduction of the foreign debt a cornerstone of the economic strategy. Consequently, the bulk of the privatization revenues from abroad was used directly to reduce the foreign debt and, hence, did not need to be sterilized. Of the US$3.8 billion in privatization revenue received in 1995 (out of a total of US$4.4 billion in foreign direct investment), some US$3 billion was used to repay foreign debt. In later years, a similarly high share of privatization revenues was used to repay foreign debt, and although the absolute amounts became more modest, privatization revenues allowed for a substantial improvement in Hungary's foreign debt position.

External debt reduction has important cost advantages as an instrument to offset the domestic impact of privatization receipts from abroad. Sterilization implies a cost to the central bank proportional to the differential between the interest rate on the debt issued and the return on foreign assets. External debt reduction does not imply such costs, and it reduces the debt-related risk premium. In the case of Hungary, however, the very success of the privatization program, and the use of the receipts for debt reduction, triggered other capital inflows and the consequent need for sterilization.

In late 1995 and early 1996, the National Bank of Hungary intervened heavily in the foreign exchange market to keep the forint from appreciating, and in the first half of 1996 sterilization took place through reverse repo operations and the sale of government bonds. As international confidence increased, and with substantial foreign investment from 1995 to mid-1998, the forint has typically been at the most appreciated edge of the band, requiring sustained foreign exchange purchases by the National Bank of Hungary and therefore sterilization operations. From March 1995 to end-1997, the liabilities of the National Bank of Hungary arising from sterilization surged from Ft 18 billion to Ft 681 billion (more than currency in the hands of the public).

---

ized enterprises decide to finance investment programs with foreign capital, as illustrated by the case of Hungary (see Box 1).[13] Substantial privatization programs may also signal favorable changes in the policy regime and in growth prospects that trigger exogenous capital inflows not directly related to the privatized enterprises. In Argentina, for example, the rapid and large-scale privatization program of the early 1990s and the use of part of the receipts to reduce public debt conveyed a signal to markets about the new policy regime that contributed to concerted flows.

Sustained capital inflows of the type discussed in the previous paragraph will contribute to the appreciation of the real effective exchange rate. Under a flexible exchange rate regime, they would result in an appreciation of the exchange rate and a reduction of inflationary pressures. Under a fixed exchange rate, or managed float, and in the absence of sterilization, such inflows would cause an expansion of base money through the increase in foreign exchange reserves, as well as inflationary pressures.

Several policy responses are available to deal with the potential destabilizing effects of concerted privatization-related capital inflows (Ariyoshi and others, 2000). Some sterilization may be necessary to smooth out and limit the effects on liquidity; however, depending on interest rate differentials, the

---

[13]Foreign-financed investment programs in privatized enterprises may contain a large import component—particularly if obsolete technologies need to be modernized—and, to that extent, the inflows would be "sterilized" through a deterioration in the external current account.

Table 4. Use of Privatization Proceeds in Case Study Countries

Country	Use of Proceeds
Argentina	Partly debt retirement, partly unearmarked budget financing.
Bolivia	Off-budget part was fully earmarked for reinvestment in the privatized public enterprises; on-budget part was unearmarked.[1]
Côte d'Ivoire	Unearmarked.
Czech Republic	Of the proceeds received by the budget, part was used for debt reduction.[2]
Egypt	During 1996–98, about one-fourth of gross proceeds went to severance pay and one-third to financial restructuring of the enterprises. The remainder was used for debt reduction.
Estonia	Initially to cover costs of currency reform (1992–93); then restitution, privatization costs, enterprise restructuring, and several extrabudgetary funds.[3]
Hungary	The on-budget share was partly used for debt retirement, while the off-budget share was used for restitution (compensation coupons), overhead of the privatization process, capital transfers to firms unrelated to the privatization process, and financing of extrabudgetary funds.
Kazakhstan	Mostly unearmarked.[4,5]
Mexico	Proceeds kept off budget were used to finance a contingency fund for debt retirement.
Mongolia	Unearmarked.[4]
Morocco	Unearmarked.[6]
Mozambique	Although most of the proceeds were used to settle the liabilities of the divested firms, in 1996 a special fund to support small-scale entrepreneurs using these resources was established.
Peru	The on-budget share was used for social spending, while the off-budget part was used to recapitalize the public pension system.[7]
Philippines	Some proceeds have been earmarked.
Russia	Unearmarked.[4]
Uganda	Severance pay to workers retrenched in the process, settlement of debts and costs of the public enterprises before sale, and promotion of entrepreneurship.
Ukraine	Unearmarked.[6]
Vietnam	The limited proceeds received so far have been reinvested in the divested firms.

Source: IMF staff.

[1]Proceeds from equity sales in the capitalization scheme were effectively reinvested in the firms divested.

[2]Vouchers, including for restitution purposes, were used for most assets divested in the early period.

[3]Vouchers were used for restitution.

[4]Vouchers were used.

[5]Some of the proceeds were earmarked for social spending.

[6]Privatization certificates were issued.

[7]The remaining proceeds have been held in a special account by the Ministry of Finance as reserves.

quasi-fiscal costs of sterilization could be significant and, in any case, must be taken fully into account when formulating policies. Real effective exchange rate appreciation may take place, depending on the exchange rate regime, through combinations of nominal exchange rate appreciation and increases in the prices of nontradables, but the use of exchange rate appreciation may be constrained by competitive considerations. Fiscal policy may need to be tightened, particularly to contain inflation and prevent an excessive appreciation of the real effective exchange rate, and especially if the flows are large relative to the absorptive capacity of the economy.

Use of Privatization Proceeds: Choices and Experience

Countries have indicated their intentions to allocate privatization proceeds to a wide variety of uses (see Table 4).[14] Below are some of the fiscal factors to be taken into account when considering the possible uses of privatization receipts.

---

[14]Assessment of whether privatization receipts were actually used in additive fashion for the intended purpose requires consideration of the counterfactual situation, for example, the amount of spending in the absence of such receipts.

Fiscal Expansion

A fiscal expansion financed through privatization receipts would generally tighten the intertemporal budget constraint. The more specific implications of higher expenditure would, however, depend on the type of spending increases that might be considered.[15]

The temporary and uncertain nature of privatization receipts suggests caution in relying on them as a source of financing of increases in current expenditure. Such increases are often difficult to reverse at some later point, and therefore there is a danger that spending may become entrenched at levels not consistent with the revenue-raising capacity of the government. If increases in current spending are nonetheless considered, their likely quality would need to be carefully evaluated.

In the short run, privatization can result in job losses and wage cuts for workers and, in those cases where price subsidies are removed, higher prices for consumers. When designing expenditure policies in a setting of large-scale privatization, it is important to address these concerns through policies to cushion the short-term social impact of privatization (see Section IV). Such policies can also increase public support for the reform process.

The fiscal stance may also be loosened through increases in domestic public investment. Particularly in countries with pressing infrastructure needs, a case could be made for implementing high-quality investment programs. Such an investment policy could aim at enhancing competitiveness by focusing on the development of infrastructure and human capital, thereby leading to higher growth. The implications of additional investment for recurrent government spending would need to be taken into account.

Government net worth would not decline as a result of capital spending if the expected return to the government on the new assets were comparable to that on financial assets. However, the conditions for this to hold are restrictive: even if public investment were to have a high return, the government would still need to capture the additional returns from the investment for it to be self-sustaining (Fischer and Easterly, 1990). Just as important, experience shows that in policy settings characterized by institutional weaknesses and constraints there is a risk that public sector projects will be poorly conceived and implemented, and that many low-return projects will end up being incorporated in investment programs.

Reduction of the Net Public Debt

The government may use privatization proceeds to reduce the net public debt by retiring debt or settling arrears, or building up financial assets, including official reserves. This occurred in several of the case study countries, including Argentina, Egypt, Hungary, Mexico, and Peru, with the debt retired being predominantly external. A reduction in the net public debt permanently lowers the fiscal deficit through a decline in net interest payments and may help reduce the exposure of the fiscal position to changes in market sentiment. In addition, the improvement in fiscal sustainability, signaled by the saving of the proceeds, could contribute to fostering market confidence and lead to reductions in the rate of interest on the public debt. The choice of whether to reduce gross indebtedness or build financial assets, and how to effect it, are debt-management issues that require appropriate consideration of relative yields; risk; the currency composition of budgetary flows, assets, and liabilities; and liquidity preference.

Some countries, including Bolivia, Estonia, and Hungary, have explicitly linked the use of privatization proceeds to the transition costs associated with a pension reform. In effect, this recognizes the implicit pension debt of the government and makes provisions for it with assets held by the state. If a government is also making efforts at maintaining or improving fiscal sustainability, the recognition of pension debt could lend credibility and help garner political support for privatization.[16]

Earmarking of Privatization Proceeds

A number of countries have formally earmarked privatization revenues (see Table 5). To some extent, the earmarking of privatization receipts may be seen as an attempt to deal explicitly with the temporary nature of privatization receipts. Under certain circumstances, such treatment of the receipts might help avoid permanent increases in spending. An element of earmarking may also be put forward to make privatization more politically acceptable, as was the case in the early stages of the Peruvian privatization process. The impact of earmarking is,

---

[15]The impact of using privatization proceeds to reduce taxes would be comparable to that of raising current spending, though clearly the distribution of the benefits would be different. If over time privatization leads to higher tax receipts, this might, however, provide an opportunity to reduce rates (see Section IV).

[16]In China, the implicit pension debt has been estimated at just under 50 percent of current GDP, and settling it has complicated efforts to reform or divest public enterprises that have substantial pension obligations to current workers or pensioners. The World Bank has suggested that one method of financing these obligations could be to use the assets of the state enterprises themselves, arguing that a portion of the implicit pension debt was accumulated as a way of financing the creation of these enterprise assets. This practice has already been implemented in a few Chinese localities (World Bank, 1997).

Table 5. Earmarking of Privatization Receipts in Selected Countries

Country	Form of Earmarking
Bolivia	Under the capitalization system, the proceeds remain in the privatized enterprises and are pledged for investment.
El Salvador	Early in 1999, legislation was passed establishing a fund to manage the proceeds obtained from the privatization of the state telephone company, under which only the interest generated by these proceeds may be spent and only in the social sectors and for the development of information centers at the local level.
Estonia	After settling debt obligations and tax arrears that were accepted by the successful bidders, some 45–50 percent of the remaining privatization proceeds were transferred to the Compensation Fund to cover its liabilities (bonds that were issued in exchange for privatization vouchers), while the remainder was earmarked to compensate previous owners of real estate.
Kazakhstan	Some of the cash proceeds from the auction of small enterprises were earmarked for social safety net purposes.
Peru	During the early stages of the privatization process, the government earmarked part of the receipts from privatization for social expenditure and structural reform programs designed in cooperation with the World Bank and the Inter-American Development Bank; inter alia, to foster public support for the privatization and reform process.
Uganda	By law, privatization proceeds are to be used to settle enterprise debts, finance retrenchment programs, meet any other costs of enterprises prior to divestiture, and promote entrepreneurship.
Vietnam	Revenues from equitization may only be used for enterprise and labor force development. [1]

Source: IMF staff.

[1] In Vietnam, equitization is a form of partial privatization of nonstrategic small- and medium-sized public enterprises. Although the mechanism was introduced in 1992, the scope and depth of equitization to date remain limited.

however, uncertain insofar as budgetary resources are fungible.

As a result of earmarking, budgetary resources, whose size ex ante may be quite difficult to predict, are placed outside the allocative budget process. Also, earmarking complicates fiscal management and makes it more difficult to reallocate spending in response to changes in circumstances or priorities, potentially forcing governments to devote more resources to an activity than they would otherwise do. Conversely, necessary spending may be constrained by shortfalls in privatization receipts. If, in addition, privatization revenues accrue to off-budget agencies and are partly disposed of outside the budget, these problems may be compounded by a reduction in fiscal control and transparency. Therefore, in general, the earmarking of privatization revenues for specific uses is not an efficient spending allocation mechanism.

Privatization, Fiscal Pressure, and Liquidity Constraints

Fiscal pressures may lead a government to privatize partly with a view to relaxing a financing constraint so as to achieve a certain level of public spending. Privatization in this case is viewed as another source of revenue—it is regarded as a windfall, and the proceeds are consumed immediately or over a longer period. This has been advanced as a hypothesis to explain privatization activity, with countries more likely to sell stakes in public enterprises if they face higher borrowing costs (Yarrow, 1999).[17]

There have been recent cases where privatization programs appear to have been accelerated—involving in some cases high-quality assets—because of the perceived need to finance deficits and support current spending in the face of financing restrictions. In Kazakhstan, the significant increase in the general government deficit in recent years—to 8 percent of GDP in 1998—was financed to an important extent from privatization receipts, which rose to more than 4 percent of GDP that year, boosted by privatization activity in the energy sector. Similarly, the fiscal policy stance in Lithuania was loosened considerably in 1998. The fiscal deficit rose by 4 percentage points to close to 6 percent of GDP, reflecting the largely off-budget spending of a surge in privatization receipts equivalent to 5 percentage points of GDP, of which the bulk was generated by the sale of the telecommunications company.

---

[17]However, some analysts, citing evidence mainly from Latin America, have argued that privatization has done little to alleviate fiscal crises (Pinheiro and Schneider, 1995).

In cases where governments embarking on adjustment and reform programs initially face financing constraints, some limited use of privatization receipts may perform a useful role. They can provide some financial cushion and fill short-term financing gaps while fiscal consolidation is effected and reforms take hold, and until confidence is restored and market access is reestablished. In the absence of an effective program of fiscal consolidation, however, such a strategy will not be sustainable.

IV   Fiscal Impact of Privatization

The fiscal impact of privatization will reflect the amount and use of the proceeds and the subsequent changes in financial flows—taxes, transfers, and dividends—to and from the budget.[18] In a broader context, consideration should also be given to the impact of privatization on quasi-fiscal costs, including subsidized credit to public enterprises. There may also be impacts on the budget from the assumption of quasi-fiscal costs that were previously imposed on public enterprises by the government arising from the pursuit of public policies, such as uncompensated provision of subsidized goods and services. Privatization often takes place as part of a policy package that involves a substantial change in the macroeconomic environment, which makes it difficult to distinguish its impact from the other effects of a regime change. Moreover, data on public enterprise operations is often scanty, and the information available on the financial flows between enterprises and the government, including quasi-fiscal flows, is less than complete.[19]

This section examines the contemporaneous impact of privatization on the budget, and its effects over time, for the case study countries. To a substantial extent, the short-run impact depends on how the privatization receipts are used, while long-run gains reflect the microeconomic benefits from exposing the enterprises to market discipline. The empirical evidence draws on the panel econometric estimates reported in Appendix II and on a less formal review of the case study experience.[20] Given the shortcom-

ings of the data, the findings on the fiscal effects of privatization need to be considered as preliminary and interpreted with particular care.

Contemporaneous Use of Privatization Proceeds

Privatization proceeds accruing to the budget may be saved or spent, the former implying reductions in domestic or external financing and the latter higher spending or reduced taxes (see Section III). These hypotheses were tested using the case study data and panel econometric techniques. To test the robustness of the findings, the effects on saving and spending were tested independently and considered for different samples and coverage of explanatory variables. The methodology and results are reported in Appendix II, with summary findings on the impact of privatization on domestic financing presented in Table 6.

The results suggest that privatization proceeds transferred to the budget are saved. More specifically, they are consistent with these proceeds being substantially used to substitute for other sources of domestic financing; the coefficient on privatization is always close to minus one and statistically significant. There is some weaker evidence for the nontransition economies that about one-fifth of the privatization receipts are used to reduce external financing, with the rest substituting for domestic financing.[21] Regressions with the overall deficit, total expenditure, and taxation as dependent variables did not provide support for the suggestion that proceeds were generally spent.

The interpretation of this econometric evidence needs to be carefully qualified, and it is difficult to assess the general applicability of these results. First, the results are based on a select sample of countries and for a limited number of years for which data

---

[18]Given the limitations of data and the problem of specifying a counterfactual, only a few studies have attempted to measure the impact of privatization on government net worth, and then only at the firm level. For the most part these have found that government net worth was increased by privatization, particularly when efficiency gains are factored in (Hachette and Lüders, 1993, and White and Kelegama, 1994). While studying the concept of social welfare, Galal and others (1994) found that in 11 of the 12 firms considered, the impact on net wealth was positive.

[19]The inadequacy of data on public enterprise operations in many countries has been documented in other studies by IMF staff as hampering analysis and policy advice. See Schadler and others (1995), and Bredenkamp and Schadler (1999).

[20]Evidence based on comparisons between the situation before and after privatization is subject to the important qualification that other events might affect the relevant variables.

[21]This reflects results from a regression with external financing as the dependent variable and is consistent with the size of the coefficient in the regression for nontransition countries in the equation for domestic financing.

Table 6. Impact of Privatization on Domestic Financing

| | Explanatory Variables[1] | | | | |
Regression	Budgetary privatization[2,3]	Overall balance[2]	External financing[2]	R-squared	Number of Observations
Full sample	−0.97 (.13)	−0.74 (.15)	—	0.54	83
Nontransition countries	−0.79 (.12)	−0.90 (.22)	—	0.50	52
Full sample	−1.19 (.19)	—	−0.65 (.20)	0.39	82
Nontransition countries	−1.03 (.11)	—	−0.96 (.19)	0.58	52

Source: Table 11.

[1]Dependent variable is the first difference of the ratio of domestic financing to GDP.

[2]Variables are significant at the 1 percent level; standard errors of estimates are in parentheses.

[3]Privatization proceeds accruing to the budget.

were available. Second, the evidence applies to the budget narrowly defined, because the sample only covers privatization proceeds identified as flowing to the budget; as discussed in Section III, there are examples of countries subject to liquidity constraints spending proceeds that accrue to extrabudgetary funds. Third, most of the countries in the sample had an IMF program for at least part of the period when privatization receipts were at their height.

If, however, the resources that are channeled through the budget tend to be saved, this would not support arguments that the placement of the privatization proceeds in extrabudgetary funds is necessary to prevent the misuse of the resources. Furthermore, the results would be consistent with the hypothesis that the formulation of fiscal plans under IMF programs is made on the basis of a deficit consistent with overall program objectives, and that privatization receipts are not a determining factor in the setting of fiscal targets, except at the margin (see Section VI).

Effects of Privatization on the Fiscal Accounts Over Time

Privatization may affect the fiscal accounts over time in several ways: directly, through its effect on financial flows to and from the privatized enterprise; indirectly, insofar as it influences the macroeconomic environment (see Section V); and as a result of decisions as to the initial use of the proceeds. This section presents evidence on developments in tax revenue, net transfers to public enterprises, more broadly defined public enterprise sector deficits, and

public debt. The partial and piecemeal evidence is consistent with the public sector in the case study countries benefiting from privatization in a longer time perspective.

Tax Revenue

Taxes paid by privatized enterprises will reflect changes in efficiency and differences in the tax regime. Increased profitability would benefit budgetary revenue, as would any intensification of restrictions to competition that favor the new owners. The impact of differences in the tax regime when an enterprise is privatized is less certain. Revenue may increase to the extent that public enterprises have sometimes been subject to less rigorous auditing and collection efforts than private firms. However, a tax system may be more difficult to administer in an economy characterized by many smaller private firms than in one dominated by large state firms whose financial operations are, in principle, transparently available to the tax authorities. Moreover, private firms may have stronger incentives to evade or avoid taxes and may also prove more skillful in doing so. In transition economies in particular, private enterprises have often proved difficult for nascent tax administrations to capture in the tax net (see Box 2).[22]

At the microeconomic level, there is evidence that privatized firms have paid higher taxes compared to the preprivatization period (Galal and others, 1994). Evidence for some nontransition case study coun-

_____

[22]For a discussion of tax issues arising from privatization in transition economies, see Kodrzycki and Zolt (1994).

Box 2. The Impact of Economic Transition on Tax Administration

The Previous system. State ownership of the productive sector significantly determined the basic practices and procedures of tax administrations in the transition countries. Under the previous system, the state was entitled to all of the profits from state-owned enterprises. Whether the state received this profit as tax revenue or as dividend payment, the total resources available to the state were the same. Moreover, because both the tax assessor (auditor) and the state-owned enterprise's tax accountant were both effectively employed by the state, their relationship was less adversarial than that between a tax auditor and the representative of a private business in a market-oriented economy. Ownership also allowed the state to make discretionary ex post changes to an enterprise's tax liabilities. In China, for example, tax authorities can still impose an adjustment tax on top of the enterprise income tax. This tax is intended to be an equalizer that compensates for differential profitability, so its rates may vary depending on the particular circumstances of each enterprise.

Another feature of state ownership is that the number of taxpayers is much smaller than in market-oriented economies. Most tax revenue is obtained from a limited number of large state-owned enterprises or collectively owned enterprises through turnover tax and profits tax. State-owned banks played a major role in monitoring the tax payments of these state-owned enterprises; for example, in some transition countries banks will still not release funds to the state-owned enterprises to pay wages until taxes due (including wage withholding) have been paid.

Changes associated with transition to a market economy. Many transition countries have continued to apply effectively the same tax assessment and collection procedures, despite the privatization of state-owned enterprises, development of a private sector, and the establishment of privately owned banks. The growing number of small enterprises, often operating outside the formal economy, has increased the burden on local tax offices considerably. For example, in Bulgaria the number of small enterprises registered by the tax administration has increased by about 100,000 each year between 1993 and 1999. In Moldova, the number of taxpayers increased from about 34,000 in 1991 to more than 350,000 in 1999, with many of the new registrants being small- and medium-sized businesses.

In all of these countries, economic transition has been a difficult challenge for tax administration. In the absence of a tax-paying culture and a willingness on the part of the tax administration to modernize procedures and systems, tax evasion and noncompliance are serious problems. Significant dollarization, continuing barter arrangements, "cash-economy" business operations, and the nascent development of the banking system have all exacerbated tax compliance problems. A number of laws, such as accounting laws, are rudimentary, complicate the work of tax administration, and increase the cost of compliance to taxpayers. Even where tax and other laws have been updated, tax officials are often poorly trained. Also, the typically low salary levels of officials in these countries may increase the risk of corruption. Finally, moribund and failing business enterprises have also created major problems for tax administration, especially when their managers give little, if any, priority to payment of taxes.

---

tries also suggests a similar conclusion.[23] In Argentina, for example, taxes paid by five large privatized firms increased significantly following privatization (Shaikh and others, 1996; see also Larraín and Winograd, 1996), while in Mexico privatized firms became significant tax contributors after having received, on average, a small net transfer prior to privatization (La Porta and López-de-Silanes, 1997). World Bank studies for Côte d'Ivoire and Mozambique also provide evidence of substantial increases in tax revenue from privatized firms.

Overall government tax revenue benefits from the likely greater efficiency of the privatized firms and the concomitant impact on growth, but it may also suffer from the increased difficulty of taxing the pri-

vate sector. The econometric results offer some limited evidence that privatization leads to a positive and ongoing increase in tax revenue as a share of GDP in the nontransition countries (see Appendix II). This increase could be due to several factors: higher collection rates from the privatized firms, either from improved compliance or enhanced administrative scrutiny; privatization leading to a shift in the structure of GDP toward sectors paying more taxes; or the privatization process coinciding with a general strengthening in macroeconomic management, including possible improvements in tax policy and administration. The fact that a majority of the sample observations coincide with the presence of an IMF program may be of importance in the context of the last factor.

Net Transfers to Public Enterprises

In many countries, the public enterprise sector has required substantial net resource flows from the bud-

---

[23]Several factors make it difficult to directly measure the extent to which privatized firms have actually paid higher taxes once divested: firms often change form—merge, restructure, disappear—after privatization; and few tax services collect information specifically on taxes paid by previously state-owned firms.

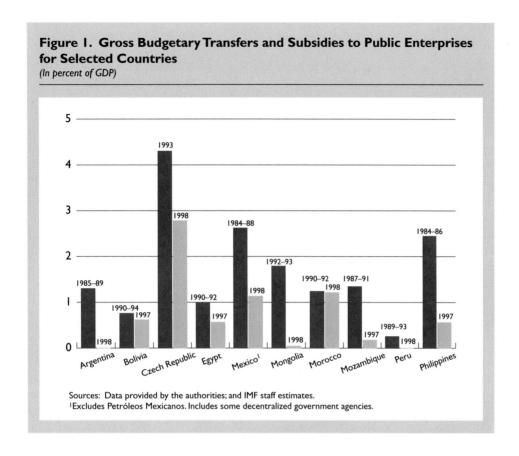

Figure I. Gross Budgetary Transfers and Subsidies to Public Enterprises for Selected Countries
(In percent of GDP)

Sources: Data provided by the authorities; and IMF staff estimates.
¹Excludes Petróleos Mexicanos. Includes some decentralized government agencies.

get over extended periods, suggesting that often the policy goals pursued through their operations are being achieved at high fiscal cost. Viewed in this way, privatization provides an opportunity to enhance the efficiency of public expenditure.

For several case study countries, gross budgetary transfers to the public enterprise sector have tended to decline with privatization (see Figure 1).[24] The reductions have been particularly significant in countries such as Argentina, the Czech Republic, Mexico, Mongolia, Mozambique, and the Philippines. In addition, there may be quasi-fiscal support to public enterprises that is not captured in the budgetary data. Public enterprises may run deficits after transfers financed by various forms of nonmarket credit, obtain "financing" in the form of insufficient investment and the corresponding deterioration of the capital stock, and benefit from government-guaranteed liabilities and tax relief.[25]

In the case study countries for which data are available, dividends paid to the budget by the public enterprise sector declined following privatization. There is often concern as to the potential negative impact on the budget of the privatization of highly profitable public enterprises. Box 3 suggests, however, that such privatization need not adversely impact the budget.

In many cases, the fiscal savings from privatization are larger than those arising from the elimination of budgetary transfers to public enterprises and above-the-line quasi-fiscal support. This is particularly likely to be the case if public enterprises record sustained deficits after such transfers, which are financed through various forms of voluntary and involuntary credit.[26] Figure 2 presents data for four countries on the overall fiscal balance of the public enterprise sector before transfers to and from the government, the amounts of net transfers, and the

---

[24]Transfers made to divested enterprises would be classified as transfers to the private sector in the budgetary accounts. There is a presumption that the scope of such transfers, if they continue to be made at all, is generally likely to be limited.

[25]For example, in Uganda, the Ministry of Finance estimated that the value of subsidies to public enterprises in 1996 amounted

to 3 percent of GDP even though direct budgetary subsidies to enterprises have been limited.

[26]Public enterprise deficits may occur in the context of normal operations and need not be indicative of a cost to the government. However, chronic deficits after transfers likely imply a large element of quasi-fiscal costs.

Box 3. Fiscal Issues in the Privatization of Profitable Public Enterprises

Sometimes there are concerns about possible negative effects on the fiscal accounts from the privatization of profitable public enterprises. In particular, the perception that it could result in revenue losses has sometimes deterred more rapid progress in privatization. The analysis of this case involves the consideration of several issues.

Profitability and efficiency. These are distinct concepts that are sometimes confused. If the private sector can increase the efficiency of a profitable public enterprise, and the government shares in these gains through the sale price and subsequent taxation, government net worth will increase even though profitable enterprises are divested.

Efficiency of privatization procedures. If profitable public enterprises are sold for less than their true value, then concerns about possible detrimental effects of privatization on the fiscal position would be warranted, but these considerations would apply equally to loss-making public enterprises.

Ability to tax. Profitable public enterprises may be a source of sizable tax receipts to the budget, but the government may be unable to tax these enterprises effectively following privatization. However, if the sales process is competitive, in principle this should be reflected in the sale price, and the tax regime should have no bearing on the impact of privatization on government net worth. Potential buyers will incorporate information about the tax regime in their offers, bidding up the price of the enterprise up to the discounted value of net earnings after tax. In effect, the government would get the net present value of the taxes forgone due to the inability to tax effectively in the lump-sum form of a higher sale price, which in turn should contribute to a lower net interest bill in the future.

Postprivatization investment and taxation. The new buyers may need to undertake investments, which, depending on the corporate income tax regime, may entail temporary effects on income tax revenue. However, if the public enterprise remained in public hands, presumably investments would also need to be undertaken at some stage to forestall decapitalization, with effects on the overall public sector balance.

Large dividends and transfers from profitable public enterprises prior to divestiture. Sometimes, when the budget gets large revenues from certain public enterprises in the form of dividends or transfers, there is a perception that as these come to an end following privatization, budget revenue will fall resulting in a deterioration of the fiscal position. However, this is a partial analysis focused solely on the budget that fails to take into account the financial position of the consolidated public sector as a whole.

One possibility is that in order to make large transfers to the budget, the profitable public enterprise is having to borrow or is decapitalizing because of insufficient investment. These preprivatization factors, which affect the fiscal position of the public sector as a whole, are not captured if the analysis focuses on the budget. Following privatization, the "borrowing" hitherto done by the public enterprise (in the form of credit or decapitalization) would just shift to the budget to make up for the loss in dividends, net of the interest that will be earned on the financial assets generated by privatization revenue.

Another possibility is that a very profitable public enterprise is able to finance large dividend and transfer payments to the budget without having to borrow or decapitalize; in the absence of such transfers, it would be building up assets. In this case, under efficient privatization mechanisms, the sale price should also reflect the enterprise's profitability, and the loss of dividends and transfers to the budget should be made up through the return on financial assets generated by privatization revenue.

Tax and interest factors to take into account in fiscal projections. The perception of a negative fiscal effect from the privatization of profitable public enterprises could arise from the failure to include appropriate estimates of the taxes expected to be paid by the privatized public enterprises in the fiscal projections, as well as the interest that will accrue on financial assets purchased with privatization proceeds, or the reduction in interest due following debt amortization financed with the proceeds.

---

balance that remained to be financed through various forms of credit. These data are for the years before the peak privatization period and for the latest year for which data are available. For these countries, both the deficit before and after transfers declined markedly following privatization, which would suggest a lessening of the fiscal burden from these enterprises.[27]

Public Debt and Interest Payments

A number of case study countries instituted explicit or implicit rules requiring that a part of privatization proceeds be directed to debt reduction. Four case study countries that expressed an explicit intention to use privatization proceeds for debt reduction (Argentina, Egypt, Hungary, and Mexico) had initial stock of registered public debt ranging between 40

---

[27]The balance of the public enterprise sector as a whole also reflects any changes that may have taken place in the financial performance of public enterprises that remain in the public sector.

Also, it is not possible on the basis of the available data to include above-the-line quasi-fiscal costs, such as subsidized interest from the banking system, explicitly into the analysis.

Figure 2. Operations of the Public Enterprise Sector Before and After Privatization for Selected Countries
(In percent of GDP)

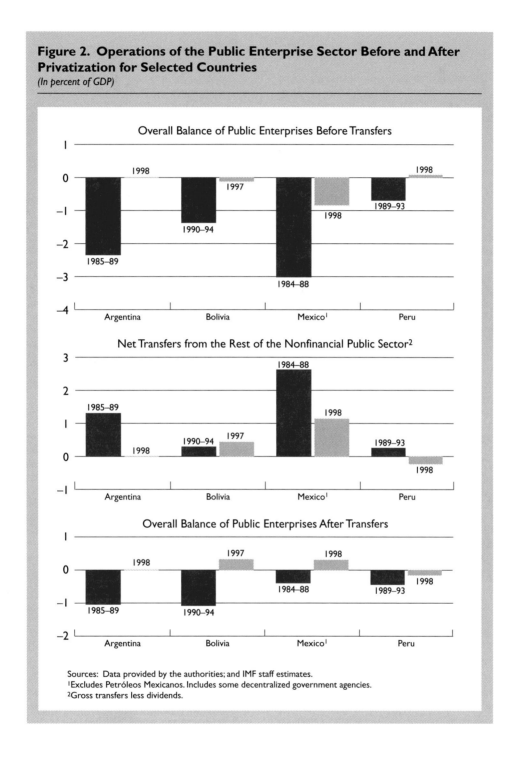

Sources: Data provided by the authorities; and IMF staff estimates.
[1]Excludes Petróleos Mexicanos. Includes some decentralized government agencies.
[2]Gross transfers less dividends.

percent and 130 percent of GDP. In each of these countries, the debt stock fell sharply between the year before the period of most active privatization and the last year of active privatization, though clearly this involved many other factors in addition to the use of the privatization proceeds (see Table 7).

In Argentina, Egypt, and Mexico, interest payments as a share of GDP fell significantly from their levels just prior to the initiation of their privatization programs. In general, where privatization proceeds were used to reduce public indebtedness, privatization contributed to the strengthening and stabilization of the economy. Thus, reductions in the interest

Table 7. Reduction in Debt Stock and Privatization
(In percent of GDP)

Country	Start of Active Privatization Period	End of Active Privatization Period	Initial Debt Stock[1]	End-year Debt Stock[2]
Argentina	1990	1995	40.1	32.0
Egypt	1993	1998	129.4	89.6
Hungary	1991	1998	66.3	60.4
Mexico	1989	1994	64.4	33.3

Source: IMF staff estimates.

[1]Stock at end of previous year, except for Argentina, where 1990 data are used because of discrepancies in the 1989 data.

[2]Stock at end of fiscal year of the active privatization period, except for Egypt, where debt data for 1997 are used.

burden are likely also to have reflected lower interest rates arising from changes in the policy regime associated with privatization. In Argentina and Mexico, significant declines in inflation rates during the period of intensive privatization also resulted in lower nominal interest rates on the domestic currency debt.

Data Issues

Many countries have experienced difficulties even forming a clear picture of the value of the productive assets they own because of data deficiencies and problems with adequate reporting. Governments should identify clearly in their accounts the revenues collected from public enterprises, including taxes paid and dividends transferred, as well as any current or capital transfers made to the enterprises. Quasi-fiscal support to enterprises should be budgetized. Efforts are also needed to improve data pertaining to the public sector fiscal position, including more adequate reporting—along with the budgetary accounts—of the operations and financing of deficits or surpluses of the sector as a whole.

V Macroeconomic Impact of Privatization

This section examines evidence of the impact of privatization on growth, aggregate investment, and labor markets and unemployment. The microeconomic evidence in each area is first summarized, then followed by econometric results from the case study countries. The measured impact of privatization on macroeconomic performance should be interpreted with caution, given the association of privatization with a broader regime change.

Effects on Growth and Investment

Economic Growth

There is substantial and growing microeconomic literature that strongly supports the notion that private firms are operationally more efficient than those held by the state. This conclusion holds for firms in competitive industries and for enterprises in less competitive settings as well, although in the latter case the conclusions may be drawn less sharply (Megginson and Netter, 1999). A wide range of studies of firm-level performance in both developed and developing countries supports this result (see Table 8), as does a recent survey of evidence for transition economies (Havrylyshyn and McGettigan, 1999).[28]

The literature on growth in developing and transition countries suggests that policy variables—particularly fiscal discipline, price and trade liberalization, deregulation, privatization, and the clarification and protection of property rights—are extremely important in determining a country's growth performance. Aziz and Wescott (1997) argue, moreover, that there may be important policy complementarities among these measures: taken individually they may have only a limited effect on growth, while conjointly they are strongly associated with rapid expansion of economic activity. Consistent with this argument, Sala-i-Martin (1997) finds that, while growth tended

to be more rapid where the share of the private sector in GDP was higher,[29] a number of the structural measures noted above tend to substitute for one another as predictors of growth. Similar results have been found in explaining growth in transition economies (Havrylyshyn, Izvorski, and van Rooden, 1998).

The data for the case study countries support these findings inasmuch as they show a significant and positive relationship between privatization and growth rates (see Appendix II). This relationship is more pronounced in the nontransition countries, but it holds for the full sample as well.[30] Privatization alone is not the suggested cause of the large increases in growth rates shown in the regressions. Rather, it is likely that privatization is serving as a proxy in these regressions for a range of structural measures that may be characterized as a change in economic regime. The results, however, are at least consistent with those on the microeconomic efficiency gains associated with privatization.

Investment

The privatization literature suggests conflicting implications for the impact of privatization on investment. Privatization should stimulate investment insofar as the management of public enterprises has been associated with significant episodes of decapitalization. The authorities, perhaps facing severe financing constraints, may have elected to forgo needed investment in public enterprises, effectively consuming a portion of the capital stock. Private purchasers of such an enterprise would need to invest significant sums to modernize the firm, driving up gross investment in the postprivatization period as a result. More generally, and over time, a positive

---

[28]The emphasis placed on speed early in the transition, particularly in the form of voucher privatization, may have come at a cost in terms of weaker corporate governance and slower enterprise restructuring (Nellis, 1999, and Stiglitz, 1999).

[29]Perotti and van Oijen (1999), moreover, present evidence that privatization serves as a positive signal for investors and that it reduces investor uncertainty over the willingness of a country's authorities to pursue prudent macroeconomic policies and to create a stable set of microeconomic incentives for investors.

[30]Havrylyshyn, Izvorski, and van Rooden (1998) discuss a variety of secular reasons why growth tended to drop sharply in the early years of transition.

Table 8. Summary of Three Studies of Firm-Level Efficiency Gains from Privatization[1]

	Developed Countries (1980s–early 1990s)	Developing Countries (1980s–early 1990s)	Developed and Developing Countries (1990s)
Profitability (net income/sales)			
Mean before privatization	0.06	0.05	0.14
Mean after privatization	0.08*	0.11*	0.17*
Share of firms with improved performance	69	63	71
Efficiency (real sales per employee)[2]			
Mean before privatization	0.96	0.92	1.02
Mean after privatization	1.06*	1.17**	1.23*
Share of firms with improved performance	86	80	79
Output (real sales)[2]			
Mean before privatization	0.90	0.97	0.93
Mean after privatization	1.14*	1.22*	2.70*
Share of firms with improved performance	75	76	88
Leverage (total debt/total assets)			
Mean before privatization	0.66	0.55	0.29
Mean after privatization	0.63**	0.50**	0.23*
Share of firms with improved performance	72	63	67
Dividends (cash dividends/sales)			
Mean before privatization	0.01	0.03	0.02
Mean after privatization	0.03*	0.05*	0.04*
Share of firms with improved performance	90	76	79

Sources: Megginson, Nash, and van Randenborgh (1994); Boubakri and Cosset (1998); D'Souza and Megginson (1999); and Megginson and Netter (1999).

[1]Statistical significance of the differences in means at the 1 percent and 5 percent levels is indicated by * and ** , respectively.

[2]Real sales and real sales per employee are normalized at 1 in the year of privatization.

impact of privatization on growth should be linked to an increase in investment.

Privatization could, however, lead to a reduction in investment to the extent that the authorities initially nationalized, or founded, public enterprises as a means of stimulating investment in domestic productive capacity. Furthermore, if these enterprises were able to borrow at subsidized interest rates, either explicitly or via an implicit government guarantee, their investment could exceed that of private firms, although this would not necessarily increase overall investment.

Megginson, Nash, and van Randenborgh (1994) found that firm-level capital expenditures, as a proportion of sales, rose significantly (by an average 45 percent) in a sample of 61 privatized firms within a set of 18 developed and developing countries. Investment increased in 67 percent of the firms they studied, with a much more significant impact on firms in competitive, rather than noncompetitive, industries. This test, when replicated for a set of developing countries, showed an even larger average in-

crease in investment of 126 percent in competitive firms across 62 percent of the firms studied (Boubakri and Cosset, 1998).[31]

At the macroeconomic level, however, no strong relationship between privatization and investment emerges in the case study countries (see Appendix II). This evidence would be consistent with the positive effect of privatization on growth being driven largely by efficiency gains.

Impact on Labor Markets

State-owned firms that occupy noncompetitive markets, or are protected through soft budget constraints, may be overstaffed and pay excessive

---

[31]D'Souza and Megginson (1999) find a much weaker relationship between privatization and investment for firms studied after privatization in the 1990s. They argue that this result obtains because many of the firms divested in the later sample were utilities that were extremely capital intensive before privatization.

Box 4. Mitigating the Social Impact of Privatization

A recent study (Gupta, Schiller, and Ma, 1999) reviewed options for dealing with the social impact of privatization.

Cushioning job losses. Employment guarantees following privatization can spread the adverse impact over a longer period, so as to allow time for the job market to become more buoyant. The drawbacks of such guarantees, however, are the likely lower sale price, which has implications for the government's ability to fund other social spending, and the more slowly realized efficiency gains, because restructuring by new owners is delayed.

Facilitating the transfer of labor to new uses. Active labor market policies can help reduce unemployment duration and shift the skill mix toward occupations in demand. Specific policies include job counseling, job search assistance, assistance and training for self-employment, and retraining.

Job creation. Sound macroeconomic and structural policies, which encourage a dynamic private sector and flexible labor markets, tend to produce strong growth in output and in employment. Public works programs can directly create jobs, but these are usually of a temporary nature, and care must be taken to ensure that the wages on offer do not discourage private sector job search.

Providing income support. Severance pay, early retirement packages, preferential allocations of shares, and unemployment insurance are possible means of support. Early retirement schemes, severance pay, and preferential share allocations can, however, impose large costs, ultimately borne by the government either directly or indirectly (i.e., through a reduced sale price). Unemployment benefits presume the existence of an effective unemployment insurance scheme, which may not be the case, especially in transition and developing economies. Moreover, coverage, the minimum contribution period, and the duration and level of benefits must be chosen carefully to minimize disincentives to employment search.

---

wages and benefits. For example, in India and Turkey in the early 1990s, overstaffing at state enterprises was estimated as high as 35 percent, while in Africa, Asia, and Latin America in the 1980s, nonwage benefits averaged 20–35 percent of the wage bill (Banerji and Sabot, 1994). Privatization of such enterprises can lead to large adjustments in employment conditions. For instance, in four Mexican steel plants 50 percent of the original labor force was eliminated during the process of privatization (La Porta and López-de-Silanes, 1997). In transition economies, nonwage benefits, such as schools and medical care, may also need to be scaled back substantially.

At the level of the firm, a growing number of empirical studies suggest that privatization is not associated with large-scale job losses. Megginson, Nash, and van Randenborgh (1994) found that, for 61 firms in 18 predominantly industrial countries, employment tended to increase after privatization. Employment levels rose in about 64 percent of the firms they studied, although in some of the cases in their sample employment had been substantially reduced prior to privatization. In a sample of developing countries, Boubakri and Cosset (1998) found a similar result, with about 60 percent of the firms in their studies experiencing an increase in employment following privatization.[32] A broader study of the macroeconomic, distributional, and employment ef-

fects of the privatization and regulation of utilities in Argentina suggested that privatization was not a major contributor to the large rise in unemployment between 1993 and 1995 (Chisari, Estache, and Romero, 1999).[33]

Privatization, particularly when accompanied by deregulation, can lead to enough new business generation that the overall level of employment in the sector rises even if employment and wages in the former state firm fall. In Zambia, for example, the liquidation of the state airline and the bus firm led to two new airlines and several new bus firms, and in both cases sectoral employment rose (Kikeri, 1998). Even if aggregate employment increases in a sector, it is possible that this reflects new entrants into that labor force, with some previous employees from the privatized enterprises remaining unemployed.

The evidence from the case study countries suggests that privatization tends to be associated with a reduction in both the contemporaneous and lagged unemployment rate (see Appendix II). As suggested earlier, it is likely that the strength of these results stems from the combined effect of many policies that are felicitous for growth and unemployment. At the same time, these results are consistent with the microeconomic evidence and do not support con-

---

[32]D'Souza and Megginson (1999), however, found a significant decline in employment for 78 privatized firms in 25 countries (of which 10 were developing countries), in a sample that in-

cluded a much higher proportion of firms in regulated industries, which were therefore less competitive and more labor intensive, than did the earlier studies.

[33]This study also concluded that infrastructure privatization and effective regulation yield significant macroeconomic benefits and gains for all income classes.

cerns as to general adverse effects of privatization on employment, at least at the aggregate level.

Even if over time privatization does not have adverse effects on sectoral or total employment, there will be workers who lose jobs on a temporary basis and, for those whose skills are more specific or who may be closer to retirement, possibly permanent effects. This lends importance to measures that mitigate the social impact of privatization, as discussed in Box 4 on page 25.

VI Issues for IMF-Supported Programs

Privatization is a reform area where the World Bank has the lead role. The privatization component of IMF-supported programs has often drawn from and supported the strategy and measures contained in World Bank–supported reform packages. IMF conditionality has reinforced public enterprise reforms, including privatization, planned under the aegis of the World Bank, where these reforms are important to the objectives of the program (Bredenkamp and Schadler, 1999). IMF staff have relied on World Bank expertise for evaluating the appropriateness and feasibility of the measures and timetables, as well as for monitoring the implementation of specific measures.

Reflecting the significant burden that public enterprises have frequently imposed on the budget and the economy, IMF-supported programs have placed growing emphasis on privatization (World Bank, 1995, and Bredenkamp and Schadler, 1999). This trend has followed from the lack of success in hardening the budget constraint of public enterprises in a number of developing and transition countries and the modest results of attempts at restructuring large enterprises and improving their operational efficiency, including through performance contracts. As a result, there has been a growing recognition that privatization may be the only way to sever inappropriate financial links between public enterprises and the government. In addition, privatization has been a key element of structural change in IMF-supported programs with countries in transition from a centrally planned to a market-driven economy.

This section examines aspects of the privatization component of IMF-supported programs approved during the period 1994–98 through a review of the case study countries, as well as the IMF's MONA database.[34] The study will be limited to programs under the SBA, EFF, SAF, and ESAF approved by the Executive Board during 1994–98.

Privatization in IMF-Supported Programs

The incorporation of privatization and privatization-related measures in IMF-supported programs has been flexible. This has reflected the underlying diversity of approaches across countries in the design of divestiture programs and supporting measures.

A large number of programs in recent years have included commitments associated with privatization (see Figure 3).[35] Monitoring has relied primarily on structural benchmarks, prior actions, structural performance criteria, and review clauses, as well as qualitative assessments of progress. The measures associated with privatization, which have been covered by IMF structural conditionality, can be classified according to the various stages of the privatization process to which they apply.

Structural conditionality associated with the privatization process has aimed at establishing the groundwork for privatization. This has often involved measures such as the preparation, approval, and announcement of privatization plans, the submission or enactment of legislation to enable or facilitate privatization, and the setting up of institutional structures and the strengthening of management needed for the privatization process. It has also involved the preparation and/or restructuring of enterprises prior to being put up for sale and actions aimed at bringing specific enterprises or groups of enterprises to the point of sale.

Conditionality attached to the pace of privatization, as measured by privatization targets, has also been used frequently in programs. Such targets have taken several forms. Most frequently, they have been

---

[34]MONA (database for monitoring IMF arrangements) has been compiled by the Policy Development and Review Department since 1993. It contains information on all IMF-supported programs under Stand-By (SBA) and extended arrangements (Extended Fund Facility (EFF), Structural Adjustment Facility (SAF), and Enhanced Structural Adjustment Facility (ESAF)) approved since January 1, 1993.

[35]The World Bank has supported privatization programs as part of public enterprise reform strategies under structural and sectoral operations in many countries. Examples of this support are provided at the World Bank website: *http://www.worldbank.org*. See also Bredenkamp and Schadler (1999).

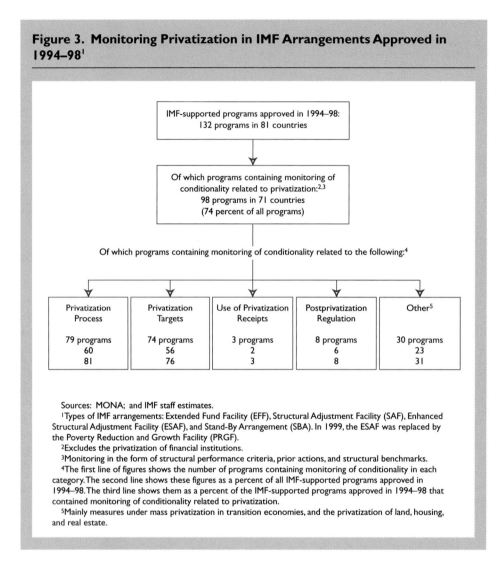

Figure 3. Monitoring Privatization in IMF Arrangements Approved in 1994–98[1]

IMF-supported programs approved in 1994–98:
132 programs in 81 countries

Of which programs containing monitoring of conditionality related to privatization:[2,3]
98 programs in 71 countries
(74 percent of all programs)

Of which programs containing monitoring of conditionality related to the following:[4]

Privatization Process	Privatization Targets	Use of Privatization Receipts	Postprivatization Regulation	Other[5]
79 programs	74 programs	3 programs	8 programs	30 programs
60	56	2	6	23
81	76	3	8	31

Sources: MONA; and IMF staff estimates.

[1]Types of IMF arrangements: Extended Fund Facility (EFF), Structural Adjustment Facility (SAF), Enhanced Structural Adjustment Facility (ESAF), and Stand-By Arrangement (SBA). In 1999, the ESAF was replaced by the Poverty Reduction and Growth Facility (PRGF).

[2]Excludes the privatization of financial institutions.

[3]Monitoring in the form of structural performance criteria, prior actions, and structural benchmarks.

[4]The first line of figures shows the number of programs containing monitoring of conditionality in each category. The second line shows these figures as a percent of all IMF-supported programs approved in 1994–98. The third line shows them as a percent of the IMF-supported programs approved in 1994–98 that contained monitoring of conditionality related to privatization.

[5]Mainly measures under mass privatization in transition economies, and the privatization of land, housing, and real estate.

quantitative—including general targets that involve a given number of public enterprises to be divested by certain dates, and enterprise-specific targets that involve certain enterprises or groups of enterprises. Targets for fiscal receipts have also been used, albeit much less frequently.

The widespread conditionality on privatization targets reflects the fundamental objective that privatization should actually take place and the often substantial drain of public enterprises on the economy and the budget. Moreover, privatization targets are more specific and more readily monitored than other aspects of the divestiture process. The need to observe announced deadlines for specific privatizations when structural performance criteria or prior actions are attached to the actual sales has the merit of emphasizing the importance attached to the sales in the program. However, this can also undermine the government's negotiating position in these oper-

ations vis-à-vis potential buyers. To guard against such an eventuality, some programs attach conditionality to the bringing of public enterprises to the point of sale, or to particular elements of the process short of final sale. In such cases, it is important to ensure, in consultation with the World Bank, that any reservation prices set by the authorities are realistic and, if possible, supported by independent valuations.

In contrast to the process and target stages in the privatization process, conditionality in the form of structural performance criteria, prior actions, or structural benchmarks has been attached much less frequently to other aspects of the privatization process. Conditionality on the specific use of privatization proceeds has been applied only in a few cases. Program ceilings, however, may be established so as to limit in effect the use of proceeds. Indeed, restrictions on the use of privatization proceeds and on the spending of proceeds in excess of programmed amounts have been included in a large number of programs through the use of quantitative performance criteria and adjusters (see below). Conditionality on postprivatization regulation through structural performance criteria, prior actions, and structural benchmarks has not been used often.

Privatization conditionality in IMF-supported programs should continue to reinforce the divestiture strategies supported by the World Bank. Within the framework of Bank-IMF collaboration, the IMF should focus on those aspects of policies—the relationship between privatization and macroeconomic policies—that are in its area of responsibility. In this regard, IMF staff should help guide reform priorities on the basis of the financial impact of public enterprises, as well as monitor budget constraints.[36]

There is room for somewhat greater selectivity in the use of structural performance criteria, prior actions, and structural benchmarks to strengthen their contribution to the success of reform. The focus, while supportive of World Bank privatization strategies, should be on privatization measures that have a significant fiscal and macroeconomic impact and that are deemed critical to the achievement of the objectives of the financial program.

The World Bank's last formal review of its assistance to privatization in developing countries emphasized the importance of focusing on the entire privatization process, rather than mainly on the number of privatized enterprises. World Bank conditionality for tranche release has subsequently been linked more strongly to the process aspects of privatization, as well as to setting up appropriate legal frameworks and regulatory institutions for the postprivatization period.

There is scope for IMF conditionality to selectively reinforce this emphasis on process and regulation where measures in these areas are considered central to the financial program.[37] This might include consideration of institutional processes; operational mechanisms for asset sales; legal and procedural changes; and the establishment of regulatory frameworks within which privatized firms, especially utilities, will operate. An increased emphasis

on process and regulation should also seek to enhance transparency and promote good governance in privatization procedures.

Conditionality on actual privatization will often remain important. This might, in some cases, be better placed in the form of structural benchmarks rather than structural performance criteria and prior actions to limit adverse bargaining incentives. Qualitative assessments, with input from the World Bank, would then be required where there are delays in specific privatizations.

Privatization and Program Design

The determination of fiscal performance criteria should reflect the macroeconomic impact of privatization proceeds and their use. From the viewpoint of fiscal control and transparency, it is important to include as broad a definition of privatization receipts as possible in the fiscal targets and quantitative performance criteria established in the program. In particular, programs should give due consideration to the extrabudgetary activities that may be associated with privatization, and these should be consolidated in the fiscal accounts. Moreover, privatization receipts should be classified as financing in the fiscal programs included in IMF arrangements. The design of programs should also take into account the expected sources of the privatization proceeds and the degree of capital mobility, particularly if the privatization program is large relative to income and monetary aggregates. As these issues were discussed substantially in Sections II and III, this section focuses on the more specific issue of the combinations of fiscal performance criteria and automatic adjusters that indicate how fiscal ceilings should change when, as commonly occurs, privatization receipts deviate from programmed levels.

The effect on the program of deviations from programmed levels of privatization receipts differs according to whether privatization proceeds are classified as revenue or financing and the nature of performance criteria and adjusters. In practice, a wide variety of combinations of performance criteria and adjusters associated with deviations from projected receipts resulting from privatization has been used in programs with the case study countries (see Table 9). Depending on the particular program, privatization-related adjusters (symmetric or asymmetric) have been attached to one or several quantitative fiscal performance criteria and to the net international reserves and net domestic assets of the central bank or of the banking system. In some cases, the applicability of these adjusters has been linked to the origin (foreign or domestic) of privatization proceeds or to their currency composition.

---

[36]Bredenkamp and Schadler (1999) discuss cases where the key aspects of public enterprise reform are not covered by ongoing World Bank activities. In those cases, it is recommended that the IMF take an active role in advising the authorities on those aspects of policies toward public enterprises that are particularly important to the financial program, in consultation with World Bank staff, until the World Bank can be more actively engaged.

[37]In Uganda, for example, the government recently revised its privatization strategy in consultation with the World Bank, and conditionality in the IMF program switched from structural benchmarks attached to quantitative privatization targets to prior actions on processes designed to bring a certain number of enterprises to the point of sale.

Table 9. Design of Adjusters Related to Privatization Receipts in Programs with Case Study Countries

Country	Arrangement[1]	Classification of Privatization Revenue in the Fiscal Accounts	Fiscal Quantitative Performance Criteria Coverage	Fiscal Quantitative Performance Criteria Concept	Adjusters Related to Privatization Receipts
Argentina	EFF 1998	Financing	Federal government	Overall balance, net disbursements of foreign and domestic debt	Measurement of net disbursements of external and domestic debt of the public sector adjusted downward (upward) for any shortfall (excess) in privatization receipts to the program
Bolivia	ESAF 1994	Revenue[2]	Public sector	Overall balance, net domestic financing	Overall balance, net domestic financing, net international reserves, and net domestic assets of central bank adjusted for privatization proceeds in excess of programmed amounts
Côte d'Ivoire	ESAF 1998	Financing	Central government	Primary balance, net bank credit	No adjusters
Egypt	SBA 1996	Financing[3]	General government	Overall balance, net domestic financing	Net domestic financing adjusted downward by the amount of privatization proceeds accruing to the government[4]
Estonia	SBA 1997	Not included (off budget)	General government	Overall balance	No adjusters
Hungary	SBA 1996	Revenue[3]	Consolidated government	Overall balance (excluding privatization receipts): quarterly performance criterion / Overall balance (including privatization receipts): annual performance criterion	Net international reserves and net domestic assets of central bank adjusted for excesses over the program baseline in cash privatization receipts from abroad
Kazakhstan	EFF 1996	Financing[5]	General government	Overall balance, net central bank credit	No adjusters
Mexico	SBA 1995	Revenue[6]	Public sector	Overall balance, primary surplus (both excluding privatization receipts), net foreign credit	Net foreign credit, net international reserves, and net domestic assets of central bank adjusted for privatization proceeds in foreign currency (excluding external debt instruments of the Mexican government)[4]
Mongolia	ESAF 1997	Revenue	General government	Net bank credit, net domestic financing	Net bank credit and net domestic financing adjusted downward for privatization revenues in excess of program baseline
Mozambique	ESAF 1996	Revenue[7]	Central government	Net bank credit	Net bank credit adjusted downward for privatization revenues in excess of program baseline
Peru	ESAF 1996	Financing	Public sector	Net domestic financing (including privatization receipts)	Net international reserves and net domestic assets of central bank adjusted for excesses and shortfalls in privatization proceeds relative to program baseline; adjusters in the event of shortfalls capped
Philippines	SBA 1998	Financing	Public sector	Public sector borrowing requirement	No adjusters
Russia	EFF 1996	Financing	Federal government	Overall balance, monetary authorities' net credit	No adjusters
			Enlarged government	Overall balance, monetary authorities' net credit	No adjusters
Uganda	ESAF 1997	Not included (off budget)	Central government	Net bank credit	No adjusters
Ukraine	SBA 1997	Financing	Consolidated government	Overall balance	No adjusters
Vietnam	ESAF 1994	Not included (off budget)	General government	Net bank credit	No adjusters

Source: IMF staff.

[1]Types of IMF arrangements: Extended Fund Facility (EFF), Enhanced Structural Adjustment Facility (ESAF), and Stand-by Arrangement (SBA). In 1999, the ESAF was replaced by the Poverty Reduction and Growth Facility (PRGF).

[2]Cash receipts. The recapitalization program is treated as off-budget investment in the firms partly divested.

[3]Only includes the privatization proceeds transferred to the government by the privatization agencies.

[4]Program baseline assumed no privatization proceeds.

[5]Until 1997: revenue; since 1998: financing.

[6]Excludes proceeds from privatization of Telmex and commercial banks.

[7]Until 1998: not included (off budget); since 1999: revenue.

Most programs were designed with the aim of preventing the use of excess privatization proceeds over the program baseline. This was achieved in a variety of ways. The fiscal deficit was capped where privatization receipts were classified as financing (Argentina, Côte d'Ivoire, Egypt, Kazakhstan (since 1998), the Philippines, Russia, and Ukraine), while in Peru the fiscal performance criterion was set on net domestic financing (including privatization receipts). In other programs, where privatization receipts were classified as revenue, adjusters limited the spending of excess privatization receipts (Bolivia, Mongolia, and Mozambique), or fiscal performance criteria were specified excluding these receipts (Hungary and Mexico).[38] However, where privatization receipts were classified as revenue, the absence of adjusters to the fiscal performance criteria implied that excess receipts could be spent by the government (Kazakhstan (1996–97)).

Programs differed somewhat more in their treatment of shortfalls in privatization receipts relative to the program baseline. In some programs, such shortfalls implied the need for fiscal adjustment (Argentina, Bolivia, Hungary, Kazakhstan (1996–97), Mongolia, Mozambique, and the Philippines), while in others privatization shortfalls could be financed, though usually up to certain caps (Côte d'Ivoire, Kazakhstan (since 1998), Peru, Russia, and Ukraine).[39]

The need to save excess privatization receipts, seen frequently in programs, is based on the principle that the fiscal program has been designed with certain macroeconomic objectives in mind and that additional nonrecurrent financial resources should be used in a manner consistent with those objectives, which typically would entail saving them. This approach is generally consistent with the discussion in Section III of the likely impact of spending additional privatization receipts on government net worth and aggregate demand.

Choices regarding program design in the presence of projected privatization receipts should be made on the basis of the fiscal and macroeconomic circumstances of the country, the objectives of the program, and the availability and timeliness of data. Judgments about types of risks to the program should also influence choices. Particular care needs to be exercised to ensure consistency between fiscal and other performance criteria. For instance, if the government must save excess privatization receipts—to the extent that this is achieved through additional deposits at the central bank—net international reserves and net domestic assets of the central bank should also have privatization-related adjusters. Otherwise, government deposits of the excess receipts with the central bank would create room for credit to the private sector to expand beyond the original program targets.

---

[38]Privatization-related adjusters were attached to the net international reserves and net domestic assets of the central bank in the case of excess privatization receipts in some of these programs (Bolivia, Hungary, Mexico, and Peru). In Hungary, the adjusters applied only to the extent that cash privatization receipts originated abroad, while in Mexico the adjusters were triggered only if the receipts were made in foreign currency.

[39]In Egypt and Mexico, the program baselines assumed no privatization receipts.

Appendix I Factors Affecting the Sale Price of State Assets

This appendix discusses elements of the privatization process that have a bearing on the sale price of assets and consequently on the resources that might be available to the budget. The material draws on the World Bank's experience and recommendations regarding privatization procedures (World Bank, 1995, and Lieberman and Kirkness, 1998). The factors that influence the sale price of assets may be classified into three broad categories according to the stage of the privatization process in which they may arise: actions taken prior to the sale of the asset, the sale process itself, and the postprivatization regime (see Table 10). Box 5 discusses related governance issues that may occur at each of these stages of the privatization process.

Actions Prior to Sale

The preparatory phase prior to privatization may include the restructuring of public enterprises. This may involve *legal* restructuring (e.g., clarification of titles and legal changes that may be required to permit private investors to acquire shares in a public enterprise); *organizational* restructuring (demonopolization or breakup); *financial* restructuring (e.g., assumption of the enterprise's debts by the government and cleanup of balance sheets); *operational* restructuring (e.g., increased investment to revamp the capital stock or closure of certain activities); and *labor* restructuring.

Legal, organizational, and financial restructuring may in some cases be essential to ensure that privatization takes place or to forestall the emergence of private monopolies. For example, the clarification of enterprise debts and legal obligations including labor issues will increase the chance of sale. The breakup of very large enterprises is sometimes needed to promote greater competition. In a number of transition economies, divestiture of social overhead functions, such as schools, clinics, and housing, was required before sale. Whether public enterprises are sold with or without their liabilities need not change government net worth. However, this could have implications for the composition and ma-

turity profile of the public debt and for the cash flow generated by the privatization and, therefore, for government liquidity.

Decisions on whether to operationally restructure public enterprises prior to privatization need to take into account the likely effect on the liquidity position of the government and on government net worth. The private sector may well be able to restructure public enterprises more efficiently than the government. Thus, preprivatization restructuring, while conceivably raising the sale price, may actually reduce government net worth.[40] Hence, additional investments to undertake the physical restructuring of public enterprises should, in general, be left to private owners once a decision has been made to privatize the enterprise (World Bank, 1995, and Lieberman and Kirkness, 1998). To the extent that a government decides to restructure firms before sale, it is important to ensure that the funds invested are subject to the same standard as for the use of any other public funds.

The issue of whether labor restructuring should be carried out by the government or left to the new owners involves difficult tradeoffs. While cases involving the need for limited restructuring are best left to the private sector, governments may consider handling large-scale redundancies prior to sale to reduce labor resistance and enhance the likelihood that a social safety net will be provided, and possibly increase the sale value. Government restructuring, however, is likely to entail fiscal costs because there may be a tendency for the state to be generous in the terms offered to the labor force to make restructuring politically and socially more acceptable (Kikeri, 1998).

The Sale Process

The state, as seller of an asset, is most likely to maximize the sale price when there are no restric-

---

[40]There is evidence that operational restructuring of public enterprises prior to privatization in Mexico was not reflected in the net sale price (López-de-Silanes, 1997).

Table 10. Factors Affecting the Sale Price: Country Illustrations

Actions prior to sale

Legal restructuring

Egypt	Legislation passed to authorize the privatization of public insurance companies.
Russia	Presidential decree issued reducing the list of "strategic" joint-stock companies that were banned from privatization.
Ukraine	Parliamentary approval required to privatize certain monopolies.

Organizational restructuring

Argentina, Bolivia	Breaking up of some public utilities into smaller units.
Transition countries (various)	Divestiture of social overhead functions.

Financial restructuring

Argentina	Treasury assumed debt of enterprises to be privatized.
Egypt	About one-third of the proceeds of privatization in FY1996/97 and FY1997/98 was devoted to financial restructuring costs.

Operational and labor restructuring

Argentina[1]	Rationalization of employment of the state oil company.
Mexico, Mozambique	Substantial investment and modernization drives.
Peru	Reduction of payroll of public enterprises and tight control of wages.

The sale process

Egypt, Mongolia, Russia, Ukraine	Limitations on the legal or effective participation of nonresidents.
Kazakhstan	High auction floor prices for small enterprises (eliminated 1996).
Mongolia	Legal restrictions established high reservation prices (abolished 1997).

The postprivatization regime

Regulation

Argentina	The telecom monopoly was largely preserved.
Bolivia	Entry to provision of long-distance and international services prohibited.
Côte d'Ivoire	Privatized telecom company granted a seven-year monopoly on some services.
Czech Republic	A 27 percent stake in SPT Telekom was sold to a consortium. SPT Telekom will maintain its monopoly status until end-2000.

Postprivatization commitments

Argentina, Bolivia, Hungary, Peru	Requirements on the amount of investment to be undertaken by the buyers.
Hungary	Purchasers required to take responsibility for environmental costs.
Mongolia	New owners required to maintain staffing levels (lifted in 1999).
Vietnam	Involuntary layoffs not permitted in first year after privatization.

Sources: Azpiazu and Vispo (1994), López-de-Silanes (1997); IMF staff.

[1]In the initial stages of the privatization process, the government placed emphasis on the speed of divestiture, and operational and labor restructuring was limited.

tions on the number of potential bidders. This would involve permitting nonresidents to participate on equal terms with residents, particularly because quite often in developing and transition countries the number of potential domestic purchasers, or the financing available to them, is limited. However, countries have sometimes placed limitations on the participation of nonresidents in the privatization process (see Table 10). In some cases, nonresidents have not been allowed to bid, or have been allowed to do so only for minority stakes in firms, while in others equity participation by foreigners has been restricted to "nonstrategic" firms. Yet "strategic" has often been defined fairly broadly, effectively serving to limit the set of potential buyers to domestic residents. Whether nonresidents are allowed to bid or

not, the process should be sufficiently open and nondiscriminatory so as to prevent noncompetitive arrangements, as occurred, for example, in the Russian loans-for-shares scheme (see Box 6).

Governments may sometimes privatize through mechanisms, such as retail offerings that may be generously priced, aimed at generating strong demand from domestic retail investors, in order to foster domestic participation in, and support for, the privatization process; create a new class of savers; and contribute to the development of the domestic capital market. In some cases, this has also involved giving preferential subscription rights to employees and other stakeholders of the public enterprises to be privatized. The pursuit of these wider objectives entails fiscal costs that need to be considered; it should also

Box 5. Governance Issues in Privatization

Privatization has been invoked as a means to combat corruption. However, the privatization process itself has often proved to be a significant source of corruption. Corrupt systems have tended to engender corrupt privatization processes and, unless accompanied by significant institutional reform, transparency has usually not benefited from privatization.

Governance issues in public ownership. Corruption, defined as the abuse of public power for private benefit, has been argued to increase with the extent of government intervention in the economy, the degree of discretion of government officials in applying regulations, the weakness of institutions and rule of law, and poor and unsystematic accountability of public officials (Rose-Ackerman, 1997). Public enterprises have been a major source of corrupt activities in many developing and transition countries (Tanzi, 1998). Such activities have included overinvoicing, accepting bribes for contracts, rationing below-market-priced goods and services through bribes, and awarding workers and managers excessively high wages and fringe benefits.

Privatization and corruption. Countries with a tradition of strong institutions, rule of law, and judicial accountability, as in western Europe, have generally engendered transparent privatization processes. In countries where privatization has been part of a comprehensive change in regime, institution building, and reorientation of the economy toward the market, such as a number of Latin American countries in the 1990s, the change in the rules of the game has, on the whole, been credible and the privatization process reasonably transparent. However, corrupt practices associated with privatization have been reported, particularly where there has been limited oversight from other branches of government (Manzetti, 1998). Where the institutional framework and rule of law have been weak, strong and well-organized interest groups have tended to "hijack" the privatization process to their advantage. This has occurred in several of the transition economies, perhaps most notoriously in the case of Russia (Åslund, 1999). The proposition that it does not matter much who gets the assets during privatization because the market soon reallocates them to efficient owners does

not seem to work in practice, partly because of the lack of capital market development in these countries.

Privatization and regulation. Since the early 1990s, a growing number of countries have started to privatize "strategic" or "core" public enterprises, such as utilities, telecommunications, transport, and energy enterprises. Problems have arisen, however, where issues related to the structure of postprivatization markets and the creation of sound regulatory regimes have not been adequately addressed prior to privatization. The major problems fall broadly into the following categories: inadequate competition, or the preservation of monopolies with no economic justification and insufficient attention to antitrust issues both before and after privatization; poorly designed regulations, or ambiguities in tariff-setting mechanisms and in the regulatory framework; and weak regulatory institutions, or the failure to prevent abuse of market power by dominant enterprises, to foster competition through the entry of new operators, and to create a favorable investment climate.

Possible lessons. First, privatization is no alternative to regulation, nor has it proven to be an impediment to rent seeking. Second, the policy of "privatizing now and regulating later" has often failed because early privatization has created strong vested interests to block the later attempts at regulation. Third, corruption significantly endangers the legitimacy of the privatization process and, more generally, weakens support for market-oriented reforms.

Therefore, privatization would be most efficient if it were preceded by institution building and the establishment of an appropriate regulatory framework and the rule of law. If the institutional underpinnings are missing but the government is making progress toward establishing them, delaying privatization until they bear fruit may be a desirable strategy. In those difficult but frequent cases where the government is unwilling or incapable of taking the necessary prior steps, the best course of action may be a cautious case-by-case, tender-based privatization with the assistance of internationally recognized financial advisors (Nellis, 1999).

---

be consistent with the key objective of efficiency gains.[41]

The choice of sales method, for example, auctions, initial public offerings, and trade sales to strategic investors, and its transparency can have important implications for the number of bidders and for the sale price. In general, auctions and initial

public offerings have served to generate higher returns than bilateral trade sales (Berg and Berg, 1997). Initial public offerings are the more common sales mechanism in industrialized countries, whereas trade sales have been more frequently used in developing countries. However, the latter are less transparent and less open to public scrutiny than more competitive processes. Moreover, they are more likely to involve significant elements of restructuring at the expense of the state as seller. On balance, therefore, it would seem preferable to rely on open auction mechanisms subject to public oversight

---

[41]The issue of mobilization of political support for privatization and the role of domestic investors have been, and continue to be, researched by the World Bank. See, for example, World Bank (1995), Lieberman and Kirkness (1998), and Shafik (1996).

Box 6. Loans-for-Shares Privatization in Russia

Following a mass privatization campaign during 1995, significant share holdings in some of Russia's largest companies—Norilsk Nickel, Yukos (oil), LUKoil, Surgutneftegaz (oil), Novolipetsk Iron and Steel, and Novorossiisk Shipping—were assigned to commercial banks as collateral for a loan to the federal government. The banks had to compete for the right to manage these assets by bidding at auction on the size of a loan to the government, but in practice only a few banks won: Uneximbank, Menatep, Stolichny, and Imperial, all of whom had close relations to the government. In most cases, the banks bid for the assets as part of a consortium, of which there were two, with the group that was politically less well connected winning none of the auctions. Foreigners were technically allowed to bid, but in practice the auctions were often set so as to ensure that the favored banks won.[1] The winner had the right to run the company until it would be sold,

again at auction, though in practice the banks themselves were generally able to acquire the assets they were managing through insider means. Six of the twelve companies were bought by the banks, which acted as auction managers, and four more were won by corporate affiliates of the firms being sold. Many of the banks that won the loans-for-shares auctions were politically active in supporting the government through the election campaigns of 1995 and 1996, while the firms that they acquired—particularly those in the energy sector—soon came to head the list of Russia's largest tax debtors.

A number of large stakes in Russian industry, particularly in the oil sector, were sold at prices that seem below their market value and in auctions that were not truly competitive. The perception that the loans-for-shares program was corrupt has weakened popular support for the privatization program overall, as well as for other market-oriented reforms.

[1]In the case of Surgutneftegaz, the auction was announced for the distant city of Surgut, where the airport was closed for two days before the auction, purportedly for weather-related reasons. Similarly, a large stake in the Norilsk Nickel conglomerate was won by a subsidiary of Uneximbank, which

also managed the auction, and which, on a technicality, had excluded a key competitor offering twice the winning bid (Lieberman and Veimetra, 1996).

whenever possible. Also, the reservation prices for assets should not be set so high that privatization is effectively foreclosed.[42]

A number of transition countries attempted to accelerate the privatization process and overcome the shortage of domestic capital by mass privatization. This mechanism involved the use of one or another form of vouchers in lieu of money. Assets were divested at little or no cost to the population, some or all of whom received a form of privatization money with which to bid on the assets for sale (Havrylyshyn and McGettigan, 1999). This form of mass privatization did not generate significant cash receipts.

The Postprivatization Regime

The key importance of setting up appropriate regulatory frameworks and institutions prior to the privatization of public enterprises with substantial mo-

nopoly power, including enterprises with network or natural monopoly characteristics, is widely recognized (World Bank, 1995). Expectations as to the extent of such postprivatization regulation can be important in determining the sale price. Firms with monopoly power that are likely to be regulated only lightly should sell for a better price than those that will be more heavily regulated. However, artificially inflating the sale price by precommitting to a lax regulatory regime would lead to a higher price at sale at the expense of potentially large efficiency costs in the rest of the economy and lower social returns over time. Moreover, countries have sometimes found it difficult to implement adequate regulatory restrictions not put in place before the firms were sold.

There is evidence in some case study countries of weak regulatory frameworks and the granting of monopoly rights in the telecommunications sector (see Table 10). These actions might have been aimed in part at enhancing privatization proceeds.

The placement of requirements on the new owners at the time of sale in the form of regulatory commitments, particularly in the case of public utilities and monopolies (for example, minimum operating standards, service levels, safety requirements, and measures to foster competition), is often warranted. Governments have sometimes placed additional requirements on buyers related to investment conditions, environmental clean up, purchase from certain vendors, and labor hoarding. Such additional re-

[42]The government may retain some "golden" share, that is, a share with special voting rights, in privatized firms—often utilities and natural monopolies. If it does so, this may lead to similar managerial and governance issues as under privatization (World Bank, 1995). However, the government's aim may be to retain the power to veto certain actions, such as takeovers, that could have the effect of asset stripping (Megginson and Netter, 1999). From the investors' perspective, the new owners may also want the government to keep a share as a form of insurance against ad hoc regulation.

quirements may reduce the sale price and could make the process less transparent. Generally, they may not be a cost-effective means of pursuing public policy goals.

An important factor affecting the amount of proceeds is the terms of payment, which may involve an extended settlement period and raise liquidity and risk management issues. In some cases, governments have not obtained payment for assets privatized in a timely fashion from buyers. This may be related to an inadequate degree of risk transfer from the government to the private sector because of the provision of generous credit terms. For example, in Uganda amendments to the Public Enterprise Reform and Divestiture statute introduced in 1997 sought to restrict extended terms of payment for enterprises privatized because of problems of nonpayment. Failure to impose discipline in this area, besides raising governance concerns, affects the effective price eventually received for the assets sold.

Appendix II   Privatization and Fiscal and Macroeconomic Developments

This appendix uses data from the case study countries to investigate the empirical relationship between privatization and various fiscal and macroeconomic variables.[43] The issues examined are whether privatization proceeds transferred to the budget are used to finance a larger deficit (spent) or to reduce other sources of financing (saved), and whether the total amount of privatization receipts is correlated with changes in macroeconomic or fiscal performance.

The sample is comprised of annual data from the 18 case study countries, using the period of active privatization for which the necessary data are available. The sample, therefore, varies between regressions due to data availability. All variables are expressed as a percent of GDP, with the exception of real GDP growth and the unemployment rate. Unless otherwise noted, the data are from the corresponding country authorities and staff estimates; the unemployment rate is taken from the IMF *World Economic Outlook* database. Finally, the country data are pooled to form the unbalanced panels that are used in the regressions.

Proceeds Transferred to the Budget

The contemporaneous relationship between privatization proceeds transferred to the budget and different fiscal variables is examined using regressions of the following form:

$$\Delta y_{i,t} = \mu_i + \delta\Delta p_{i,t} + \beta\Delta x_{i,t} + u_{i,t}, \qquad (1)$$

where Δ is the first difference operator, $y_{i,t}$, $p_{i,t}$, $x_{i,t}$, and $u_{i,t}$ are, respectively, the dependent variable, privatization proceeds, an additional explanatory variable (if included), and the residual; subscripts refer to the value for country i in period t. The parameters to be estimated are μ_i, which is the country-specific or fixed effect, δ, and β. The hypothesis that privatization proceeds transferred to the budget are spent is tested by examining the statistical significance of

δ using the overall balance, total expenditure and net lending, and total revenue as the dependent variables. The saving hypothesis is tested using domestic financing, external financing, and government debt as the dependent variables.

The empirical results are consistent with privatization proceeds being saved, specifically that they substitute one-for-one with domestic financing (see Table 11). This conclusion is robust and is not fundamentally altered by changing the sample or adding explanatory variables. Moreover, it is supported by the findings that privatization proceeds are not used to increase the deficit, increase spending, or lower revenue.[44] For the nontransition sample, there is some evidence that about one-fifth of privatization receipts are used to reduce external financing, with the rest offsetting domestic financing. These results need to be qualified by recognizing that the regressions are based on a limited sample, largely comprised of observations that coincide with periods when the country had an IMF-supported program;[45] and, by design, only budgetary privatization proceeds are included, leaving open the question of what happens to amounts not transferred to the budget.

Total Amount of Privatization

The correlation between the total amount of privatization receipts, which better indicates the switch from private to public ownership, and variables, such as growth, unemployment, and tax revenue, is examined using regressions of the following form:

---

[43]A fuller description of methodology and results is available on request from the authors.

[44]Results from the spending and revenue regressions are not shown. Also, regressions using the debt stock as the dependent variable suggest that it is independent of the amount of budgetary privatization proceeds. This likely reflects noise in the debt-to-GDP ratio due to movements in nominal GDP growth rates and financing operations that affect the debt stock without impacting the recorded deficit.

[45]A formal test of the proposition that budgetary privatization proceeds are only used to reduce domestic financing when there is an IMF-supported program is rejected. There are, however, limited observations without an IMF-supported program, and in some such cases a program may have been under discussion.

Table 11. Contemporaneous Impact of Budgetary Privatization Proceeds on Domestic Financing [1]

	Full Sample			Nontransition			Short Sample [2]		
	(Dependent variable: first difference of domestic financing)								
Δ Budgetary privatization (t)	−1.14* (.19)	−.97* (.13)	−1.19* (.19)	−.85* (.13)	−.79* (.12)	−1.03* (.11)	−1.20* (.23)	−1.12* (.15)	−1.21* (.23)
Δ Overall balance (t)	n.a.	−.74* (.15)	n.a.	n.a.	−.90* (.22)	n.a.	n.a.	-.46* (.17)	n.a.
Δ External financing (t)	n.a.	n.a.	−.65* (.20)	n.a.	n.a.	−.96* (.19)	n.a.	n.a.	−.10 (.26)
Observations: R-Squared	83 .19	83 .54	82 .39	52 .17	52 .50	52 .58	26 .41	26 .64	25 .46
	(Dependent variable: first difference of the overall balance)								
Δ Budgetary privatization (t)	.25 (.19)	.22 (.20)	.31 (.20)	.09 (.11)	.10 (.11)	.09 (.12)	.22 (.28)	.15 (.36)	.32 (.26)
Δ Real GDP growth (t)	n.a.	.03 (.04)	n.a.	n.a.	−.02 (.02)	n.a.	n.a.	.09 (.25)	n.a.
Δ Unemployment (t)	n.a.	n.a.	−.24*** (.12)	n.a.	n.a.	−.20 (.14)	n.a.	n.a.	−.44 (.46)
Observations: R-Squared	89 .12	88 .12	81 .16	58 .13	57 .14	51 .15	28 .01	28 .03	24 .09

Sources: Data provided by country authorities; and IMF staff estimates.

[1]Standard errors are in parentheses and based on White's (1980) Heteroskedasticity-consistent covariance matrix. Asterisks indicate significance levels: * is 1 percent level; ** is 5 percent level; *** is 10 percent level. Except for the short sample regressions, in which a constant is included, the regressions include a complete set of country-specific dummies for which the estimates are not reported. All variables are expressed as a share of GDP.

[2]Comprises observations corresponding to the two largest movements in privatization proceeds for each country.

$$\Delta y_{i,t} = \mu_i + \delta p_{i,t} + \gamma p_{i,t-1} + \beta \Delta x_{i,t} + u_{i,t}, \qquad (2)$$

where the notation is the same as before. In equation (2), the first difference of the dependent variable is run on the level of privatization.[46] The dependent variable, therefore, is assumed to follow a random walk with drift during the sample period, and privatization is now allowed to have either a lasting or one-period ($\delta = -\gamma$) effect on the dependent variable.

There is some evidence of a positive and lasting impact of privatization on tax revenue for the non-transition sample, but not for the full sample (see Table 12). This may reflect higher collection rates from the privatized firms, a shift in the structure of GDP toward sectors paying more taxes, or a general improvement in macroeconomic management. Privatization receipts are also found to be strongly correlated with a lasting improvement in macroeconomic performance, as manifested in higher real growth and lower unemployment. Given the simple specification that is used, the results should be interpreted cautiously and not construed to imply causation. Moreover, the privatization variable is likely capturing the positive impact of a general regime change toward better economic policies. Finally, the evidence from regressions (results not shown) using fixed investment as the dependent variable suggests that it is not correlated with privatization.

---

[46]When real GDP growth is the dependent variable, it is included in levels, and its lagged value is added as an additional explanatory variable.

Table 12. Structural Relationship Between Total Privatization Proceeds and Selected Variables[1]

	Full Sample					Nontransition				
(Dependent variable: first difference of tax revenue)										
Privatization (t)	.16 (.17)	.16 (.17)	.15 (.17)	n.a.	n.a.	.28** (.12)	.27** (.13)	.26** (.11)	n.a.	n.a.
Privatization (t − 1)	n.a.	−0.15 (.15)	−.23 (.16)	n.a.	n.a.	n.a.	.05 (.11)	−.02 (.09)	n.a.	n.a.
Δ Privatization (t)	n.a.	n.a.	n.a.	.16 (.11)	.18 (.12)	n.a.	n.a.	n.a.	.11 (.10)	.14*** (.08)
Δ Unemployment (t)	n.a.	n.a.	−.11 (.07)	n.a.	−.10 (.06)	n.a.	n.a.	−.24** (.10)	n.a.	−.24** (.10)
Observations:	104	104	83	104	83	69	69	49	69	49
R-Squared	.26	.27	.28	.27	.28	.17	.18	.27	.14	.24

	Full Sample				Nontransition			
(Dependent variable: real GDP growth, in percent)[2]								
	LSDV		Anderson-Hsiao		LSDV		Anderson-Hsiao	
Privatization (t)	1.07** (.49)	1.01** (.46)	.37* (.13)	.55* (.12)	1.96* (.53)	1.82* (.57)	.72* (.21)	1.11* (.20)
Privatization (t − 1)	n.a.	.71** (.36)	n.a.	.35* (.12)	n.a.	1.09** (.50)	n.a.	1.12* (.20)
Real GDP growth (t − 1)	.05 (.11)	.01 (.11)	.15* (.03)	.13* (.03)	−.35** (.14)	−.41* (.14)	−.25* (.04)	−.26* (.04)
Observations:	107	107	90	90	70	70	60	60

	Full Sample					Nontransition				
(Dependent variable: first difference of the unemployment rate)										
Privatization (t)	−.27*** (.15)	−.25*** (.13)	−.21** (.10)	n.a.	n.a.	−.12 (.10)	−.28** (.14)	−.27** (.13)	n.a.	n.a.
Privatization (t − 1)	n.a.	n.a.	−.50* (.19)	n.a.	n.a.	n.a.	n.a.	−.16 (.18)	n.a.	n.a.
Δ Privatization (t)	n.a.	n.a.	n.a.	.14 (.12)	.13 (.11)	n.a.	n.a.	n.a.	−.08 (.07)	−.06 (.10)
Real GDP growth (t − 1)	n.a.	−.03 (.06)	.02 (.05)	n.a.	−.04 (.06)	n.a.	.13** (.06)	.14** (.07)	n.a.	.10*** (.06)
Observations:	86	86	86	86	86	50	50	50	50	50
R-Squared	.15	.16	.24	.14	.15	.18	.25	.26	.17	.23

Sources: Data provided by country authorities; and IMF staff estimates.

[1]Standard errors are in parentheses and based on White's (1980) Heteroskedasticity-consistent covariance matrix. Asterisks indicate significance levels: * is 1 percent level; ** is 5 percent level; *** is 10 percent level. The regressions include a complete set of country-specific dummies for which the estimates are not reported. The Anderson-Hsiao estimator, however, takes first differences to remove the country dummies prior to estimation. Except for real GDP growth and the unemployment rate, all variables are expressed as a share of GDP.

[2]The combination of a lagged dependent variable and country-specific dummy (i.e., fixed effect) may lead to estimates that are biased using ordinary least squares (LSDV). Although the Anderson-Hsiao estimator avoids this problem, such alternative estimators may not provide better estimates of the coefficients on the privatization terms, and thus both results are reported (Judson and Owen, 1997).

References

Anderson, T.W., and Cheng Hsiao, 1982, "Formulation and Estimation of Dynamic Models Using Panel Data," *Journal of Econometrics*, Vol. 18 (January), pp. 47–82.

Ariyoshi, Akira, and others, 2000, *Country Experiences with the Use and Liberalization of Capital Controls*, IMF Occasional Paper No. 190 (Washington: International Monetary Fund).

——Åslund, Anders, 1999, *Why Has Russia's Economic Transformation Been So Arduous?* paper prepared for the Annual World Bank Conference on Development Economics, Washington, April.

Aziz, Jahangir, and Robert F. Wescott, 1997, "Policy Complementarities and the Washington Consensus," IMF Working Paper 97/118 (Washington: International Monetary Fund).

Azpiazu, Daniel, and Adolfo Vispo, 1994, "Some Lessons of the Argentine Privatization Process," *CEPAL Review*, Vol. 54 (December), pp. 129–47.

Banerji, Arup, and Richard H. Sabot, 1994, "Wage Distortions, Overmanning and Reform in Developing Country Public Enterprises," Vice Presidency for Finance and Private Sector Development (Washington: World Bank).

Berg, Andrew, and Elliot Berg, 1997, "Methods of Privatization," *Journal of International Affairs*, Vol. 50 (October), pp. 357–90.

Beyer, Hans-Joachim, Claudia Dziobek, and John Garrett, 1999, "Economic and Legal Considerations of Optimal Privatization—Case Studies of Mortgage Firms (DePfa Group and Fannie Mae)," IMF Working Paper 99/69 (Washington: International Monetary Fund).

Boubakri, Narjess, and Jean-Claude Cosset, 1998, "The Financial and Operating Performance of Newly Privatized Firms: Evidence from Developing Countries," *Journal of Finance*, Vol. 53 (June), pp. 1081–110.

Bredenkamp, Hugh, and Susan Schadler, eds., 1999, *Economic Adjustment and Reform in Low-Income Countries* (Washington: International Monetary Fund).

Chisari, Omar, Antonio Estache, and Carlos Romero, 1999, "Winners and Losers from the Privatization and Regulation of Utilities: Lessons from a General Equilibrium Model of Argentina," *World Bank Economic Review,* Vol. 13 (May), pp. 357–78.

D'Souza, Juliet, and William L. Megginson, 1999, "The Financial and Operating Performance of Privatized Firms During the 1990's," *Journal of Finance*, Vol. 54 (August), pp. 1397–438.

Fischer, Stanley, and William Easterly, 1990, "The Economic of the Government Budget Constraint," *The World Bank Research Observer*, Vol. 5 (July), pp. 127–42.

Galal, Ahmed, and others, 1994, *Welfare Consequences of Selling Public Enterprises: An Empirical Analysis* (New York: Oxford University Press).

Gupta, Sanjeev, Christian Schiller, and Henry Ma, 1999, "Privatization, Social Impact, and Social Safety Nets," IMF Working Paper 99/68 (Washington: International Monetary Fund).

Hachette, Dominique, and Rolf Lüders, 1993, *Privatization in Chile: An Economic Appraisal* (San Francisco: International Center for Economic Growth).

Havrylyshyn, Oleh, Ivailo Izvorski, and Ron van Rooden, 1998, "Recovery and Growth in Transition Economies 1990–97: A Stylized Regression Analysis," IMF Working Paper 98/141 (Washington: International Monetary Fund).

Havrylyshyn, Oleh, and Donal McGettigan, 1999, "Privatization in Transition Countries: A Sampling of the Literature," IMF Working Paper 99/6 (Washington: International Monetary Fund).

Heller, Peter S., 1990, "The Budgetary Impact of Privatization: Examples from New Zealand and Prospects for Ireland," in *Privatization: Issues of Principle and Implementation in Ireland*, ed. by Frank J. Convery and Moore McDowell (Dublin: Gill and Macmillan).

——, and Christian Schiller, 1989, "The Fiscal Impact of Privatization, with Some Examples from Arab Countries," *World Development*, Vol. 17 (May), pp. 757–67.

Heller, Peter S., Richard Hemming, and Ruba Chakrabarti, 1997, "Macroeconomic Constraints and the Modalities of Privatization," in *Fiscal Policy and Economic Reform,* ed. by Mario I. Blejer and Teresa Ter-Minassian (London: Routledge).

Hemming, Richard, and Ali M. Mansoor, 1987, "Privatization and Public Enterprises," IMF Working Paper 87/9 (Washington: International Monetary Fund).

International Monetary Fund, 1986, *A Manual on Government Finance Statistics* (Washington: International Monetary Fund).

Jones, Leroy P., Yahya Jammal, and Nilgun Gokgur, 1998, "Impact of Privatization in Côte d'Ivoire," report prepared for the Privatization Committee, Boston Institute for Developing Economies, Boston, November.

Judson, Ruth A., and Ann L. Owen, 1997, "Estimating Dynamic Panel Data Models: A Practical Guide for

Macroeconomists," Finance and Economics Discussion Paper Series 97/3 (Washington: Federal Reserve Board of Governors).

Kikeri, Sunita, 1998, "Privatization and Labor: What Happens to Workers When Governments Divest?" World Bank Technical Paper No. 396 (Washington: World Bank).

Kikeri, Sunita, John Nellis, and Mary Shirley, 1992, *Privatization: The Lessons of Experience* (Washington: World Bank).

Kodrzycki, Yolanda K., and Eric M. Zolt, 1994, "Tax Issues Arising from Privatization in the Formerly Socialist Countries," *Law and Policy in International Business*, Vol. 25, pp. 609–37.

La Porta, Rafael, and Florencio López-de-Silanes, 1997, "The Benefits of Privatization: Evidence from Mexico," NBER Working Paper 6215 (Cambridge, Massachusetts: National Bureau of Economic Research).

Larraín R., Guillermo, and Carlos D. Winograd, 1996, "Privatisation massive, finances publiques et macro-économie: Le cas de l'Argentine et du Chili," *Revue économique*, Vol. 47 (November), pp. 1373–408.

Lieberman, Ira W., and Rogi Veimetra, 1996, "The Rush for State Shares in the 'Klondike' of Wild East Capitalism: Loans-for-Shares Transactions in Russia," *The George Washington Journal of International Law and Economics*, Vol. 29, pp. 737–68.

Lieberman, Ira W., and Christopher D. Kirkness, eds., 1998, *Privatization and Emerging Equity Markets* (Washington: World Bank).

López-de-Silanes, Florencio, 1997, "Determinants of Privatization Prices," *Quarterly Journal of Economics*, Vol. 112 (November), pp. 965–1025.

Mackenzie, George A., 1998, "The Macroeconomic Impact of Privatization," *Staff Papers*, International Monetary Fund, Vol. 45 (June), pp. 363–73.

Mansoor, Ali M., 1993, "Budgetary Impact of Privatization," in *How to Measure the Fiscal Deficit: Analytical and Methodological Issues*, ed. by Mario I. Blejer and Adrienne Cheasty (Washington: International Monetary Fund).

Manzetti, Luigi, 1998, "Are Market Reforms Ending Corruption in Latin America?" *Mondes en développement*, Vol. 26, pp. 69–81.

Megginson, William L., Robert C. Nash, and Matthias van Randenborgh, 1994, "The Financial and Operating Performance of Newly Privatized Firms: An International Empirical Analysis," *Journal of Finance*, Vol. 49 (June), pp. 403–52.

Megginson, William L., and Jeffry M. Netter, 1999, "From State to Market: A Survey of Empirical Studies on Privatization," draft paper prepared for joint conference of SBF Bourse de Paris and the New York Stock Exchange, Paris.

Nellis, John R., 1999, "Time to Rethink Privatization in Transition Economies?" *Finance and Development*, Vol. 38 (June), pp. 16–19.

Newbery, David M., 1997, "The Budgetary Impact of Privatization," in *Fiscal Policy and Economic Reform*,

ed. by Mario I. Blejer and Teresa M. Ter-Minassian (London: Routledge).

Perotti, Enrico C., and Pieter van Oijen, 1999, "Privatization, Political Risk and Stock Market Development," CEPR Discussion Paper no. 2243 (London: Centre for Economic Policy Research).

Pinheiro, Armando Castelar, and Ben Ross Schneider, 1995, "Fiscal Impact of Privatization in Latin America," *Journal of Development Studies*, Vol. 31 (June), pp. 751–85.

Rose-Ackerman, Susan, 1997, "The Political Economy of Corruption," in *Corruption and the Global Economy,* ed. by Kimberly A. Elliott (Washington: Institute for International Economics).

Sala-i-Martin, Xavier, 1997, "I Just Ran Four Million Regressions," NBER Working Paper 6252 (Cambridge, Massachusetts: National Bureau of Economic Research).

Schadler, Susan, and others, 1995, *IMF Conditionality: Experience Under Stand-By and Extended Arrangements, Part I, Key Issues and Findings*, IMF Occasional Paper No. 128 (Washington: International Monetary Fund).

Shafik, Nemat, 1996, "Selling Privatization Politically," *Columbia Journal of World Business*, Vol. 31, pp. 20–29.

Shaikh, Hafeez, and others, 1996, *Argentina Privatization Program: A Review of Five Cases* (Washington: World Bank).

Stiglitz, Joseph E., 1999, *Whither Reform? Ten Years of the Transition*, paper prepared for the World Bank Annual Bank Conference on Development Economics, Washington, April.

Tanzi, Vito, 1998, *Corruption Around the World: Causes, Consequences, Scope, and Cures,* IMF Working Paper 98/63 (Washington: International Monetary Fund).

Verbrugge, James A., William L. Megginson, and Wanda L. Owens, 1999, "State Ownership and the Financial Performance of Privatized Banks: An Empirical Analysis," paper presented at the World Bank/Federal Reserve Bank of Dallas Conference on Banking Privatization, Washington, March.

White, Halbert, 1980, "A Heteroskedasticity-Consistent Covariance Matrix Estimator and a Direct Test for Heteroskedasticity," *Econometrica*, Vol. 48 (May), pp. 817–38.

White, Howard, and Saman Kelegama, 1994, "The Fiscal Implications of Privatisation in Developing Countries: The Sri Lankan Experience," Institute of Social Studies Working Paper No. 179 (August), pp. 1–38.

World Bank, 1995, *Bureaucrats in Business: The Economics and Politics of Government Ownership* (Washington: Oxford University Press).

———, 1997, *Old Age Security: Pension Reform in China*, China 2020 series (Washington: World Bank).

Yarrow, George, 1999, "A Theory of Privatization, or Why Bureaucrats Are Still in Business," *World Development*, Vol. 27 (January), pp. 157–68.

Recent Occasional Papers of the International Monetary Fund